The Internal Development Necessary to Become Loving & Wise

Dr. Paul Hatherley

BALBOA.
PRESS
A DIVISION OF HAY HOUSE

Balboa Press books may be ordered through booksellers or by contacting:

Balboa Press
A Division of Hay House
1663 Liberty Drive
Bloomington, IN 47403
www.balboapress.com
1-(877) 407-4847

Printed in the United States of America

ISBN: 978-1-4525-3915-7 (sc)
ISBN: 978-1-4525-3916-4 (hc)
ISBN: 978-1-4525-3917-1 (e)
Library of Congress Control Number: 2011915868

Balboa Press rev. date: 09/20/2011

CONTENTS

Part II: Understanding & Nurturing Internal Needs

Part III: Thinking For Understanding & The Seven Mental Tools

Foreword

Have you ever wondered, "Just what is human nature, and where does it come from?" In reviewing history, it is obvious that people have been more concerned with trying to control survival and security than learning how to develop love and wisdom. In trying to get survival and security under control, we have been intensely competitive, and often tried to exploit one another to gain temporary advantages. One sad result is that we have come to think of fear and greed as *just human nature.*

Throughout history, some people have become loving and wise, and these people we tend to revere as saints or deities. Jesus, Buddha, Lao Tsu, Confucius, Gandhi, etc. are familiar examples of people we have seen as special, or even as deities because of their degree of love and wisdom. There is also the occasional person in our everyday acquaintance that seems to embody the qualities of love and wisdom, and we often admire, respect and feel warmly toward these people.

As much as we respect, admire, or even worship people who integrate love and wisdom, we have yet to establish (at least as far as I am aware) the training necessary so that people who want to become loving and wise can learn the required skills and awareness. Instead, our daily priorities and purposes indicate we value survival and security, while love and wisdom are relegated to beliefs, assumptions or ideals that we revere; but so far, have failed to clearly define and consciously master.

What I am suggesting is that it is time to make becoming loving and wise both a *practical goal* and a *conscious purpose* in our everyday lives. To make developing love and wisdom a practical goal, we must have a sequential process defined by observable facts, specific skills and concrete activities—not just vague feelings or fantastical beliefs. Too often, people imagine that love and wisdom are a consequence of how they *feel*, or what they *believe,* rather than a *factual* development of their minds and emotions created by mastering specific skills and concrete activities.

The purpose of this book is to provide the information everyone needs to master his ***objective*** *internal needs and potentials, as well as* ***specific*** *mental tools necessary to think for understanding, and a* ***concrete process*** *for building genuine emotional bonds.*

Each category provides *complex sequences* of skills and awareness necessary to build love and wisdom. With the mental and emotional development created by mastering these sequences, we become empowered to fulfill both our *universal* and *unique* needs and potentials. Becoming loving and wise is one consequence of this fulfillment.

I have identified the processes necessary for internal growth through a lifetime of reading, personal observations, and professional experience. Essentially, my life has been devoted to pursuing the answer to one question, "What, if anything, will make human life *internally* satisfying and genuinely meaningful?"

Through books I have scoured history, literature, philosophy, and psychology looking for the answer to my question in the lives, emotions, thoughts, and imaginations of Western civilized experience. I have also explored the thoughts, lives, emotions, and experiences of Eastern philosophers and spiritual leaders.

For twenty-five years, I practiced traditional psychotherapy, and for the last ten years have taught the awareness and skills necessary for mental and emotional development. Through studying people who became loving and wise, as well as those who did not, I have identified *universal* needs, potentials, and mental tools that every internally developed person I have ever studied has to some degree understood and mastered.

What anyone can easily observe is the internal development of a few people is not enough to change the history of human beings. While we are better off having a few wise people to provide examples rather than having none, it is also clear that each ordinary person needs to master internal development in his own way, and for his own purposes. It boils down to the old cliché that it is better to *teach someone how to build his own house, rather than give him one that is already completed.*

Certainly, simple observation of the daily plight of human beings around the globe would indicate that the existence of a few, or even many loving and wise people has not trained the rest of us to be loving and wise. Instead, we tend to either ignore or pervert the teachings of the great personages of human history. It seems that we simply cannot live in a house of love and wisdom that someone else has built, but must learn how to build our very own abode.

The initial skills and awareness necessary to build love and wisdom are presented in **Part One,** the *Five Internal Potentials.* These internal potentials are universal for all human beings, and every internally developed person I have studied has to some degree mastered all five. Fulfilling the *five universal potentials* leads to an internal growth that is neither mystical nor magical. Instead, these potentials are easily observed *possibilities* that common sense will tell you are essential to developing your mind and emotions. The five potentials are: ***Understanding, Caring, Mastery, Creativity, and Contribution.***

Each potential identifies sequences of skills and awareness necessary to build layers of insight that over time grow into love and wisdom. For instance, in mastering our potential to **understand**, we learn how to observe, think, and *see in detail* every critical relevant truth. Through this process, we learn how to see and understand our perspective *(motivations, needs, purposes, choices and behaviors).* One valuable lesson we learn *through understanding perspective* is that our unique experience of life is separate from that of our mate, children, and friends.

Developing a *desire* to understand ourselves, life, and other people requires that we master the second potential—**Caring**. ***While understanding develops our consciousness, caring provides the "desire" to use our newfound awareness to become loving and wise.*** Together, the desire generated by caring, and the insights acquired by understanding, create the critical layers of internal development necessary to master every human need and potential. It is important to note that when we fail to grow the primary reason is always the same—we lack the caring necessary to generate a wholehearted desire to grow!

Mastery ***is the third universal potential, and provides the skill we need to apply the insights acquired with understanding, and energized by caring.*** Mastery is a critical potential because everyone needs the skill, awareness, self-worth, and internal power created by becoming competent. We can easily observe that the basic requirements for acquiring any kind of competence—internal or external—is to first *define*, then *practice*, and eventually *master* specific skills and awareness.

The fourth potential—**creativity**—extends and expands mastery into expressing a unique vision of our love for life. After using understanding and caring to master our *universal* needs and potentials, we need to develop our *unique* talents. Most people are impatient and want to jump into being creative without first mastering their basic needs and potentials. ***This impatience insures we produce only the mediocre expressions of an insecure ego, rather than express the authentic creativity of an original consciousness.***

Finally, to fulfill our internal potentials requires becoming competent to C**ontribute.** There is no activity more effective in providing an enduring expression of love and wisdom than becoming competent to contribute to the experience and lives of other people, Mother Nature, and eventually to the collective consciousness and caring of the entire species.

Benjamin Franklin, a well-known and wise American, consciously formed his life around *contributing* to the benefit of the people around him. Benjamin said he wanted his legacy to be that he was *useful* to other people, rather than he *died a rich man*. In reading about his life, we quickly see that Benjamin consciously worked to master all five universal human potentials.

In **Part II**, we define the most important internal needs. A *need* is distinguished from a *desire* by the fact that if we fail to gratify a desire we experience disappointment, but no real damage. By contrast, if we fail to feed a need, then we experience some degree of real damage to our mind, emotions, or body. Understanding our needs is essential to feeding them.

It is important to notice that ***acquiring enough internal development to feed needs and fulfill potentials in our personal, professional, and relationship lives is a critical source of internal happiness.*** Nothing in life is either healthy or happy if its needs and potentials are not fed and fulfilled. Simply look at the trees, plants, flowers, birds, and animals to see if anything is truly healthy, happy, or complete if its needs are not satisfied and its potentials not fulfilled.

While flowers and trees are not subject to being *consciously* happy or unhappy, we still think of them as "unhappy" when their needs are not satisfied. This is why we often speak of plants and trees as "looking sad" when they are brown and droopy rather than green and vibrant.

Animals will both look and act unhappy when they cannot fulfill their potentials, like in a zoo when they are captive and cannot move about freely. In captivity, even when their external needs for food and shelter are adequately satisfied, their internal needs for stimulation, mobility, and challenge are denied and the animals clearly suffer, just like you or I would. (It is important to note that we often deny an animal's internal needs, similar to how we often deny our own!)

Of course, suffering, like happiness is experienced in degrees. So, animals in a zoo suffer *internally* from a loss of freedom, variety of experience, and purpose. On the other hand, they are not *externally* abused or intentionally made miserable. Wherever on the scale of happiness/misery you currently reside, understanding needs and potentials will help you observe and measure the degree of happiness/ misery you have created.

The ultimate source of love and wisdom is to master being able to *understand and nurture* ourselves, life, and other people. In normal life, we are not trained in how to see ourselves and other people accurately, define internal needs and potentials, or how to *think* until we *understand* our own and everyone else's perspective. Instead, we are taught to pursue success and security, and to acquire impersonal information that leaves us anxious about our self-worth, unable to build bonded relationships, and still in the dark as to how to define *conscious purposes* that give our lives direction, structure, and meaning.

Now, in **Part III**, we present the bedrock foundation for all understanding in *thinking for understanding and the seven mental tools*. When we master the seven mental tools, then we also become internally competent to explore everyday reality and learn what is true, define what is needed, and teach ourselves how to feed every real need. This training is essential because it provides the foundation for learning how to *understand and nurture* ourselves and other people, which just so happens to be a handy initial *working definition for learning how to love and become wise.*

Finally, in **Part IV**, we define the internal need many people are obsessed with, but often unable to satisfy—building bonded relationships. In this section, we present the key elements necessary to build emotional bonds*: personal conversation, conscious touch, and sharing reality, purposes, and quintessential moments.*

Historically, every increase in human understanding has created real improvements in everyday life—beginning with learning how to control fire and use it for cooking and heat. People improved life again by learning how to grow food and store it, rather than depend on hunting and gathering. Then, inventing the wheel and making sophisticated tools and weapons made life even more comfortable and secure.

In addition to making external life more comfortable, people have also progressed socially and culturally. In advancing civilization, we have created language, law, and writing. We have also organized ideas and beliefs to create religion, politics, and philosophy. However, to view human evolution in perspective, we must acknowledge it was only in the last century that we passed laws to protect children from industrial exploitation. It also took until the 20th century to establish the 40-hour workweek, give women the right to vote, and make racial discrimination both illegal and immoral.

If we are to continue this *internal* evolution then we must *consciously* acquire all the awareness and skills necessary for our mental and emotional development. One happy consequence of internal growth is that we learn to care more about *understanding and nurturing* than *competing and exploiting*. At this point in history, we desperately need the internal competence essential to *understanding and nurturing* all life on planet Earth—plants, birds, animals, fish, and other people.

The current need for internal development is urgent because an epidemic exists of individual crises in terms of endless addictions, as well as anxiety, overweight, unsatisfying relationships, depression, and widespread apathy. We also suffer global problems with insufficient resources, over-population, unstable economies, climate change, and chronic political conflicts.

To solve the personal issues that damage our individual lives, and the global problems that threaten our existence, requires a degree of internal development, understanding, and ability to work co-operatively that does not now exist. Our only hope is for large numbers of people to want mental and emotional development for their own happiness, as well as to solve the global issues that challenge and threaten all human beings.

In the following pages are the concrete internal skills and awareness everyone needs to build his own house of love and wisdom, and in the process develop his mind and emotions to a degree of subtlety and sophistication not offered in normal life. It is important to notice that mental and emotional development is necessary to integrate not only love and wisdom into our everyday experience, but also internal happiness.

When you read this book it might help to study it like a textbook rather than read it like a novel. I have been told that it contains an intense concentration of information that requires energy and a focused mind to understand and assimilate. Other than careful studying, all you need to bring to the party is a whole-hearted commitment to explore, learn, integrate, and apply the information.

PART ONE:

Five Internal Potentials

Connecting Love & Wisdom With Internal Happiness

Imagine that you wake up on the first day of your long awaited and much anticipated ski trip in a comfortable condo with glorious mountain views, a stone fireplace hosting a crackling cozy fire, a hot cup of coffee, and 12 inches of fresh powder outside the window that promises perfect skiing. Sounds wonderful, doesn't it? (Feel free to substitute a sun saturated beach in the Bahamas if that is more to your taste.)

Now, imagine you are alone, but really want to be in the company of someone you love. This discontent may introduce a degree of sadness, and perhaps anxiety. Or, imagine you are with someone, but the relationship is conflicted because both of you want more attention, energy, or approval than the other has to give. Or imagine that you are very insecure about your skiing, and are just competitive enough to be anxious about how you will perform on the slopes.

What you can see is that *internal* conflicts, anxieties, and discontents are quite capable of diminishing or even ruining *externally* perfect experiences. Everyone knows the powerful ruining effect that internal anxieties, hungers, conflicts and disappointments can have in daily life. What everyone does not know is how to create the satisfaction, meaning, consciousness, caring, and competence necessary to become genuinely and completely happy—whether the external circumstances are perfect, or not!

This example offers a powerful insight into one reason that real and enduring happiness is often so elusive. That is, most of us expect something *external* will make us happy, and never do learn that no matter how perfect or controlled we make our external surroundings, real happiness requires we also define and master our *internal* needs and potentials.

The problem in normal life is that almost all our attention and training focuses on mastering the external. Our training begins early. We often start by learning in a peewee league to compete *to win* in soccer, baseball, football, or even ballet class. In high school, we compete for grades, usually so we can get into a good college and go on to a high paying job, or become a successful entrepreneur. It is normal to assume that success in our professional lives will inevitably lead to also being happy in our personal and relationship lives.

Nowhere in normal life are we taught to acknowledge *internal* needs and potentials, and then receive direct, specific, concrete, and effective training in how to *be a conscious and caring person, satisfying mate, competent parent and real friend*. Real happiness requires having enough *external* wealth to feed our material needs—and enough *internal* development to master our mental and emotional needs so we can become loving and wise.

Internal development is the pivotal issue for human beings at this juncture in our history. Right now, every critical external issue requires a degree of internal development that as a group, human beings simply do not have. One consequence is that the problems and needs of our times overwhelm our ability to accurately observe the facts, consciously think about what they mean, and painstakingly discover what is required to solve our problems and feed our needs. This is as true for the large global issues threatening our political and economic stability and prosperity, as well as the small individual issues that diminish or destroy our personal fulfillment and significant relationships.

What most needs changing is our purpose. When we are taught, and subsequently believe that happiness will occur as a result of becoming externally successful, we make it our purpose to acquire *control* over creating a pleasant and comfortable life. With this *normal* purpose defining our priorities, we do not even try to understand and nurture ourselves and other people. Instead, we try to control every pain and pleasure.

Creating internal happiness requires a totally different purpose. The *conscious* purpose we need is to respond to the mystery and marvel of being alive by wanting to *explore and understand* all the positive and negative experiences that life offers. With a *conscious purpose* to explore and understand, we expand our attention to include all the external and internal facts, needs, potentials, problems, and responsibilities that life inevitably drops into our unsuspecting laps.

Internal happiness has been a rare experience for human beings, in part, because few people adopt the required *purposes*. In addition to lacking conscious purposes, there is no training in normal life for how to develop our minds and emotions so we can build the love and wisdom necessary for internal happiness. ***Simply put, internal happiness requires that we first adopt a conscious purpose to explore life in its entirety; then we must master our internal needs and potentials, the seven mental tools, and the process necessary to build emotional bonds.***

It is important to notice that mental and emotional development takes time and effort, as well as repetition and practice. Because we learn some things quickly and easily, we often assume we should learn all things quickly and easily. Internal development is one activity that I have never seen anyone (including myself) learn quickly or without focused effort. If you engage this process with a purpose to become loving and wise, you will create a clearly defined and life-affirming goal that provides a renewable source of energy and inspiration.

By the way, even if you are a person who unconsciously protects your right to be anxious, critical, or chronically discontent, it is important to note that even this set of attitudes and behaviors can be changed by education, time, and effort. Just because you were trained to be neurotic (anxious, depressed, conflicted or divided) does not mean that it has to be a life sentence. Quite the contrary, you can start from wherever you are now and build a new and life-affirming character, or improve the old one by acquiring information, practicing new habits, and developing internal skills.

Defining Internal Happiness

To begin, *internal* refers to every experience that takes place in our minds and emotions. This means that thoughts, feelings, beliefs, ideas, theories, desires, fears, expectations, etc. all qualify as "internal" experiences that occur inside our heads and hearts. (Just as a matter of interest, emotions and thoughts both come from our minds; the "heart" we often refer to as the source of feelings is just a metaphor.)

The second word we need to define is *happiness*. This word is difficult because it points to complex experiences that are both subjective and objective. As a result, one person may be *happy* spending his life as a teacher, while other people may want to be a forest ranger, fireman, doctor, welder, etc. These preferences are *subjective* and *unique* to each person, so there is no better or worse. In the past, people have assumed that happiness is an entirely subjective and unique experience, and then used this assumption as an excuse to avoid exploring the issue to discover whether or not there may be *objective* and truly *universal* aspects to internal happiness that can be defined, taught, and learned.

Over the past thirty years, I have explored the experience of internal happiness and discovered certain *universal* requirements. For instance, two requirements necessary to become mentally and emotionally (internally*)* happy, are that we must develop consciousness and caring. The purpose for this development is to replace the normal tendency to *obsess over feelings* with consciously learning how to *observe, think, and learn*.

You may ask, "What makes consciousness and caring *universal* requirements for internal happiness?" Well, can you imagine being internally happy when you are chronically hungry for experiences you cannot even define, much less provide? Or, can you imagine being internally happy when your emotions are divided and you feel anxious, confused, or needy for approval?

By contrast, one consequence of internal development is that we become competent to feed needs and fulfill potentials. In the process, we also become whole-hearted, so our caring is focused. In addition, we build genuine self-worth, so we no longer waste time obsessing about how we feel about ourselves, or what other people think about us, but instead, create the satisfaction that comes from being both internally and externally *competent.* If you had this degree of development, does it seem that you would also create some degree of internal happiness?

Now, take it a step further and ask, "Can I imagine that anyone who masters internal development and becomes loving and wise would *inevitably* experience some degree of internal happiness?" If this seems reasonable, and you test this insight by observing people in everyday life, as well as in books and movies, you will see that consciousness and caring are *universal* requirements for building happiness.

Next, if you use this process to define and fulfill your internal potential to become a *satisfying mate, nurturing parent, and real friend*; is it obvious that you will expand and enhance your experience of internal happiness? On the other hand, can you see that if you pass through life unaware and uncaring, unable to fulfill yourself, satisfy a mate, nurture a child, or care for a friend, then you cannot be internally happy?

Mental Requirements for Internal Happiness

Happiness is built; it does not just appear spontaneously because you are a "good" person. Instead, happiness is built on understanding, and understanding is built in your mind—one observation, question, and insight at a time. We can all imagine "epiphanies of awareness" creating a spontaneous rush of cosmic enlightenment! No work and no waiting. It happens immediately, and without effort. Sounds great to me! Only problem is that spontaneous rushes of cosmic enlightenment do not, and cannot happen.

Everyone's mind can be developed, but incrementally, not instantaneously. Translated, this means our minds grow slowly via one observation, question, and insight at a time, or not at all. This insight may be disappointing, but check it out against your actual experience before you avoid, argue, or explain it away.

What makes understanding so critical is that internal happiness can only be built on feeding needs and fulfilling potentials. This means that our potential to be conscious and caring, the pre-requisites to love and wisdom, are internal developments that require a genuine connection to real-world experience.

How do you *consciously* connect to everyday experience? The most direct way is to pay attention to every small and ordinary event, and make *accurate observations.* Then, you need to ask *intelligent questions* and create *useable insights.* If you fail to pay attention and make accurate observations, and instead define reality in terms of beliefs and feelings—then you remain forever unaware and disconnected from actual experience.

It is true that we can become competent to make a living, but remain inadequate to see reality accurately in our personal and relationship lives. Sadly, this uneven development happens frequently in our culture. One reason is that we all acknowledge the need to survive, and often rely on the rational process of *observing, thinking, and learning* to function at work, but in our personal and relationship lives unconsciously rely on the normal neurotic process of *obsessing, feeling, and fantasizing.*

Building internal happiness and becoming loving and wise requires that we explore everyday life until we *understand* what is true and master our needs and potentials. This is what makes *observing, thinking, and learning* so critical; that is, we need to observe reality accurately so we can build internal happiness in every part of life—personal, professional, and relationships.

Emotional Requirements for Internal Happiness

With normal training, our energy goes into *controlling* security, self-image, success, and enjoyable entertainment—rather than wholeheartedly wanting to *explore* the mystery of being alive so we can become loving and wise. This means that in normal life we are soon taught to pursue *control* over pain and pleasure and rarely develop any real interest in *exploring* life so we can master living; in part, because the reward is not immediately obvious, and none of our friends are doing it!

On the other hand, if we *care* more about exploring life than controlling pain, then we create a source of energy we can use to master internal needs and potentials. With the insight from exploring, and the energy from caring, we are prepared to work as hard as necessary to become loving and wise.

Not *wanting* to work is the next biggest obstacle to internal development. We often believe that internal development and happiness should just happen, so we should not have to work to develop our minds and emotions. Try challenging this common assumption by observing ordinary people in your acquaintance, as well as famous people you read about, until you see how seldom, in spite of external success, anyone becomes conscious, caring, competent and internally fulfilled, (much less loving and wise) and it will be apparent that if you want internal happiness, then you must ***work for it***.

One source of motivation to do the work necessary to master internal development is to observe that without the meaning that is a natural consequence of becoming loving and wise, then external success quickly becomes empty and unsatisfying. The reason is that at the end of the day, we all have a painfully short life span and need to experience the *ultimate satisfaction* of a truly meaningful life. No meaning, no happiness.

There are more emotional requirements necessary to pursue internal development, but these three are sufficient to begin. That is, all development requires *whole-hearted caring, an innocent desire to explore life, and a conscious commitment to work*. Of course, as we continue to grow, we also need the *courage* to acknowledge facts, tolerate uncertainty, and risk change.

Sensual Requirements for Internal Happiness

The source of all connection to experience is our senses (sight, sound, taste, touch, smell). To verify this statement imagine what it would be like to have all your senses suddenly and completely shut down. What would be the effect? Or imagine an infant who has never known life and has no memory, but does have a mind and is deprived of all sensory information. Can you imagine this infant's experience? Sounds like a nightmarish plot for a "can't get it out of my head" horror movie, doesn't it?

If you think about the critical role your senses play in just making everyday experience possible, it may become obvious that your senses also play a critical role in internal development. Now, we must ask the obvious question: "What are the sensual requirements for internal development?"

The two most important sensual requirements are simple; we must *receive and remember* our sensual experiences. Consciously receiving and remembering sensual experience is necessary to create multiple *points of contact* between ourselves and the experience of being alive. One sign of internal growth is when we expand the number and quality of our points of contact to ourselves, nature, and other people.

One technique for learning how to expand your points of contact is by reading about people who made consciously connecting to everyday experience their life's work. For instance, read the work of the poet, Emily Dickinson, or the teenage diary of Anne Frank, or the American naturalist, John Muir, and you will discover that each person had many points of contact with both nature and other people.

Also, John, Anne, and Emily used every point of contact to *observe, think about, and learn from* the sometimes delightful and occasionally horrifying experience of just being alive—and then artfully described his/her unique experiences in an original and creative manner. If you study the work of these three people, you may discover that each in his/her own way was *internally* happy, even though the *external* circumstances in each person's life were far from perfect.

Learning from Anne, Emily, & John

If you read Anne Frank's diary, Emily Dickinson's poetry, or John Muir's accounts of his experiences in nature, you will see that all three developed sensual awareness. Anne Frank was only a teenager whose life was first interrupted by having to hide in a small attic in Holland for three years during World War II. Then, discovered by the Nazis when she was still only 15, she was shipped off to Auschwitz to die before turning 16.

In spite of these awful external circumstances, Anne passionately observed nature, even when all she had to view for three years was a single tree outside her window and a tiny view of the sky. When being shipped to the concentration camp in a cattle car, Anne was excited to be outside, and she observed the passing countryside through a slit in the wood slates with a child's delight.

If you read Anne's diary, you will see a young girl observing herself, her parents, sister, and the other people in the attic with a desire to explore the mystery of being alive. By paying attention to ordinary experience, as well as every conversation, attitude, and behavior in her little group, Anne acquired a degree of wisdom. One thing she learned was how to *live alone* in her own thoughts and feelings—because no one else in the attic was conscious or caring enough to share with. Anne is not alone in needing to heed this lesson!

John Muir also had a highly developed and sensually based consciousness backed-up by whole-hearted caring for nature and life. This life-affirming response to being alive was developed in spite of the fact that his father was mean, and treated John cruelly. John did his best to fulfill his potentials in the punishing home environment, but as soon as possible set off to make his own way in the world. John Muir was immensely talented, and could have been enormously successful as a businessman/inventor in the external world.

Instead, John pursued a love of Nature and spent his time consciously exploring life in extraordinary places and with wild creatures. He made it his purpose to first understand and then protect the ultimate source of human energy and inspiration—the natural world. John Muir fulfilled his own potential to live fully and completely, while leaving in his wake the legacy of a man consciously connected to the raw beauty and wildness of walking alone through a pristine Nature that he did his best to experience and preserve.

Emily Dickinson is rated by some as the foremost American poet, and yet, after her late twenties rarely left her father's home in Amherst. Emily preferred her own company because, like Anne Frank, she discovered that other people were not interested in observing, thinking about, and learning from life and living. Her experience of Nature was limited to her back yard (about an acre of land), and yet, she was intimately and sensuously connected to the little creatures she found there, as well as to sunrises and sunsets, the changing seasons, and the sweet and often inspiring company of trees and flowers.

Emily did have contact with other people, and through them explored the depths of life and love. Like Anne Frank, Emily became wise by looking long and deeply into what other people would consider a small slice of life. Her understanding of life was detailed, deep, and delightfully original. Nothing escaped Emily's notice, and she invariably discovered the kernels of life and meaning that quietly hide inside every seemingly ordinary experience.

The *external* circumstances of John, Emily, and Anne's lives were enormously different, but their *internal* responses are remarkably similar. All three consciously absorbed many sensuously based *points of contact* with life and nature. All three were internally developed in their ability to observe everyday experience, think about what they saw, and learn the unique and universal lessons life is always ready to teach. Reading about John, Anne, and Emily will introduce you to people you can learn from and share with who are no longer breathing, but yet, are still vibrantly alive!

Points of Contact & the Four R's

Connecting to experience is critical to fulfilling our potential to be conscious and caring, which as you know, is a requirement for internal development and eventually, happiness. Emily, Anne, & John all knew how to consciously connect to being alive. The process they used, each in his/her original way, can be defined in terms of the Four R's—*receive, remember, reason and respond.* This is an easy-to-memorize process that once mastered will enhance and expand your sensual, mental, and emotional points of contact with every experience.

The first step to enhancing experience is to concentrate your consciousness and whole-hearted caring on *receiving* the information from your senses. This means that whether at home, on vacation, in nature, or in a business park, you give whole-hearted attention and carefully note everything your senses report. One result of paying attention is that you become intensely aware of the constantly changing degrees of beauty, ugliness, warmth and coldness in the environments around you.

The next step is to *remember* what you see, hear, taste, touch and smell. All animals have some awareness of their sensual experience, but animals *remember* little of what they experience. You might ask, "How much of my sensual experience do I remember?" and "Does it seem to be more, or less than what I imagine the average chipmunk remembers?"

Remembering sensual experiences is essential because memory provides both the information and time we need to apply the third R—*reason*. We need *reason* to make connections between past and present events, causes and effects, and one experience to another. We also need reason to derive the *meaning* of what we see, hear, taste, touch and smell. When we *consciously* go through the process of receiving, remembering and reasoning, we are prepared to *respond.*

Our first response may be to simply describe the experience. Next, we may experience feeling inspired, repulsed, saddened, delighted, or joyful. Then, we need to use reason to make connections so we can learn something new from each experience, or confirm something we already understood. Finally, we may use what we have learned to develop a new skill, or change an idea, attitude, or behavior.

Following the Four R's, we consciously connect to everyday life and other people. Conscious connections to life are essential to create the long-term fulfillment and meaning necessary to first become loving and wise, and over time—internally happy.

Defining the Potential To ***Understand***

Consciously exploring everyday experience for the purpose of *understanding* ourselves is a strictly human potential. Other animals can react to what is in front of them, sometimes with thought, but they cannot *imagine* an experience and *consciously connect* facts to consequences, or past to present. Nor can other animals *extrapolate* by using insight gained from one experience to understand another experience with similar characteristics.

These differences between human beings and other animals create a quantum difference in the degree of *understanding,* or *consciousness* that each can develop. It is important to note that consciousness for humans is only a *potential!* Without training, most people go through life with little understanding of their own internal needs and potentials, much less the perspectives of other people, animals, or nature.

One way to measure the quality of our *consciousness* is by observing the degree of detail and depth in what we *understand.* Understand what—anything and everything—but especially our own perspectives. Someone's perspective is defined by his *motivations, purposes, needs, wants, choices and behaviors.*

Just for fun, take a moment and try to define precisely what *motivated* you to choose your career, mate, or to have children. Can you identify the motivations that inspired each choice? Next, did your choices actually feed your needs, fulfill your potentials and provide satisfaction, or something else? On reflection, do you think you understood your internal needs and potentials? Have you understood anyone else's needs and potentials? Does it seem that more *understanding* would be helpful?

Answering these questions will help in identifying how well you can define and understand your own perspective. Is an accurate measure of your self-understanding information you genuinely want, or would usually tend to avoid?

Seeing in Detail

Seeing facts accurately and in detail is the first step in *understanding* any need, topic or event. To *understand* the human body, for instance, people began by observing skin, muscles, and bodies in motion in order to map basic physiology. Later, we dissected cadavers. At first, we just wanted to ***see*** the innards ***in detail,*** and then we wanted to learn how all the parts function and interact with each other.

The process of understanding the complexity of the human body began with simply observing the surface facts. Next, we dug deeper and looked inside to acquire even more layers of information. We have continued to explore the structure and function of the human body until today our understanding has evolved into *seeing* in ever greater *detail* the intricacies and interactions of our own bodies.

We still do not thoroughly understand the human body, but we know a whole lot more than when we started. It is important to notice the ***process*** we used. As we have seen, understanding any issue or topic requires that we begin by examining the surface, so in choosing to learn about our bodies, we began by observing skin, muscles, and bodies in motion.

Next, to further our understanding we needed to *dig down* and explore our subject in more detail. The initial purpose was to see how our bodies work—but very soon we wanted to *understand* disease and healing. Historically, most of our motivation to understand the human body has been fueled by a desire to heal disease.

This means that in the beginning, our purpose was to *control* the *negative* experience of disease, rather than *master* the *positive* experiences necessary to create health. Mastering positives has been until recently only a side issue for the science of medicine. To genuinely ***understand*** our bodies, we must learn how to both *control the negative* (heal disease), **and** *master the positive* (create health).

What this example from the science of medicine reveals is that ***understanding*** anything requires that we follow a ***process***. The first step in the process is to simply observe the pertinent facts until we see the surface in detail. This means we begin by observing the most easily observed facts of whatever it is we want to understand. Once we observe the surface, we need to dig down and learn more—layer by layer, and one detail after another.

Positive & Negative

Historically, people began the process of exploring the unknown by trying to ***understand*** the negative. Medicine is a good example because for most of history people have chosen to limit their inquiry to the goal of healing disease, and only recently have vigorously engaged the problem of how to create health. It is important to note that we usually begin any and all explorations motivated by a desire to *control negatives*.

In trying to maintain a healthy weight, for instance, we usually think in terms of what ***not*** to eat. We often believe that if we *control the negative* of what not to eat, then our weight loss will happen automatically. The problem is that even if we avoid the "bad" foods we will still **not** create the energy and health provided by mastering diet and exercise.

On the other hand, if we both eliminate the *negative* of eating unhealthy food, and master the *positive* of eating a nutritious diet and add exercise to our daily lives, then we will attain our ideal weight ***and*** create energy and health.

Another example of trying to control negatives occurs every day in how we respond to close relationships. Whether with a child, mate, or friend, we often try to *control the negative* created by interpersonal conflict rather than *master the positive* of building emotional bonds. We usually fail to even think about a relationship unless there is a crisis. It is simply not part of normal life to master offering personal conversation, or learn how to share conscious purposes, reality, and quintessential moments in order to build emotional bonds with the people we love.

It is important to remember that the process necessary to understand anything begins with observing facts until we see a specific issue or topic in detail. Next, we must explore both the negative and positive aspects of our topic. The complete process of first "seeing in detail" and then exploring both positive and negative dimensions is required to build a true understanding of any issue, topic, need or potential.

Understanding Ourselves

We have just seen that *understanding* begins with observing the surface facts and proceeds by digging down into our subject until we see all the significant details, as well as all the causes and consequences of every positive and negative characteristic. Of course, we need a way to focus our observations, and this is where intelligent *questions* become necessary.

In trying to understand ourselves, one question first proposed by mystics is quite helpful in focusing our study. This ancient question is simply, "Who am I?" This is a powerful question that we normally go through a lifetime and never once ask, or answer. Anyway, let's have a go at it.

At a basic level, one answer to this ancient question is, "I am a trainable nervous system . . ." Then, if we are over the age of 12, we can add, " . . . that has already been trained!" This observation has significant ramifications. For one, if at the core of who we are is a *trained nervous system*, this means we have already acquired a personality full of mental and emotional habits and patterns that pre-determine how we think and feel, as well as our overall response to the fact of being alive.

As we look at all the mental and emotional habits and patterns that define us, another intriguing question pops up; that is "Once my nervous system has been trained, ***can I retrain it***?" Of course, my answer is a resounding, "Yes, you can!" but in fact, this is a question every person must explore and discover the answer to for themselves.

After defining the basement level answer to *who am I*, the next layer acknowledges the self-evident facts that define each person. That is, the life of every person who has ever lived, or ever will live, begins and ends with the same equipment: *a mind, body, emotions, and lifespan*. No matter what other optional equipment we possess; like whether we are pretty or plain, smart or stupid, rich or poor, lucky or born under a "bad star", every human shares these four facts. If we observe these four facts in everyday life, we soon see that each person's mind, emotions, and body come pre-equipped with *needs* and *potentials.* Observing how we *respond* to our needs and potentials; whether we *consciously* master every single one and become personally fulfilled and internally happy, or *unconsciously* react and become internally conflicted and unhappy, or just muddle through trying to feel good will add yet another layer of understanding to help in answering the question, "Who am I?"

We have simply been *making observations and asking questions* for the purpose of creating layer upon layer of insight into ourselves. Now, to continue the process of exploring the question, "Who am I?" we will employ the universal human potentials: *Understanding, Caring, Mastery, Creativity, and Contribution,* so we can ask even more questions that additional layers of insight.

For instance, if we ask, "What do I *understand* about my internal needs and potentials, and how detailed is my *understanding?"* we can see to what degree we are *conscious* of our internal development, which is helpful in assessing precisely what we have learned, and still need to learn. With normal training, we rarely assess our understanding of internal needs and potentials.

Next, we need to ask, "What do I *love,* and when and how well do I *express* my love?" This question helps assess to what degree we have fulfilled our potential to *Care*, which is an enormous insight into seeing who we really are, as opposed to the person we imagine ourselves to be, or would like to be. To assess our degree of caring, we need to define the word in terms of experience. For instance, *caring can be defined as **wanting** to commit time, energy, and effort to a task, person, or experience.*

Now, re-ask the question, "What do I care about, or love?" and observe the people, objects, or activities where you devote whole-hearted energy and effort over time, and in addition, willingly suffer for when the need arises. With this criteria in mind ask again, "What do I really care about, or love, and how competently and consistently do I express my love?"

The next question, "What have I *Mastered*, and to what degree has it brought me satisfaction and meaning?" is both enlightening and dangerous because it may generate a bad feeling or two. It is important to notice that one requirement for all internal development is the willingness to tolerate bad feelings in the service of seeing what is true.

When observing what you have mastered try not to be too obsessive by defining *mastery* as being synonymous with *perfect*. Mastery just means that you have put effort and energy into learning something difficult and you can do it "pretty well." One thing you want to look for in understanding yourself is to see the breadth, depth, and range of your interest in life as measured by your attitude toward mastery. For instance, do you consciously look for things to be interested in and learn about? Or, are you more passive and mostly only engage activities that come easily and require little effort, commitment, and energy?

Another way to measure your degree of internal fulfillment is to ask, "To what degree have I become *Creative* in how I live, work, relate, and renew?" This is a complex and multi-layered question that requires time and effort to adequately answer. Being creative in how you live, work, relate and renew requires you first become original and authentic, and then focus your energy and thought on each activity until you become internally as well as externally competent. When you answer these questions innocently and honestly, you can see yourself with more accuracy, and assess in detail the degree of your internal development. One *principle of life* that helps to alleviate any anxiety you may have at discovering the truth about yourself is that *as your awareness grows, so do your options.* This means that the reward for tolerating a few bad feelings is that you are released from the prison of normal anxiety and oblivion and allowed to walk freely into the fresh air and energizing sunlight with the option to experience life, grow, and learn. As a result, once you know ***who you are,*** you are empowered to intelligently choose who you ***want to be***!

Understanding Perspective—

Motivations, Purposes, Needs, Choices & Behaviors

Have you ever wondered "What in God's name *motivated* me to marry that person . . . buy that house or car . . . make that investment . . . etc?" Or, have you ever wondered how you could have acquired every success life offers, and yet still feel incomplete, or suffer from a vague feeling that something—you don't know exactly what—is missing? Or have you ever wondered what it would take to make your mind peaceful, your emotions whole-hearted, your relationships satisfying, and your work meaningful—but been unable to find the answers?

At one time or another most people ask these and many other important questions about themselves or life, and find they cannot answer them. Once you understand perspective: *motivations, purposes, needs, choices and behaviors*; you will be able to answer all these questions, and more. For instance, when you can clearly define all five categories of your perspective, you will understand the *process* you follow when you make rational choices, as well as the sometimes embarrassing irrational ones!

When you understand perspective, you will not only be able to observe yourself accurately, but also other people, close and distant. You will see in detail precisely what made a particular relationship satisfying, as well as how it became distant, or conflicted. As a result, you will understand what is needed to reduce conflict, or increase intimacy. In other words, *understanding perspective* is one of the most powerful tools in creating the internal development necessary to become loving and wise.

Motivation

Motivation is something that is often mysterious to us, which is why in reminiscing people say, "Gosh, I don't know why I did XX!" Rarely do we observe that motivation is tied to needs, wants, priorities, and purposes. Instead, motivations are usually *unconscious,* which frequently makes them somewhere between difficult to impossible to accurately observe, or clearly define.

We can begin by defining motivation, the first element in understanding perspective, as **the *energy generated by feeling fear, desire, longing, caring, or experiencing a real need—internal or external.*** You can verify the truth in this definition by observing ordinary experience. For instance, if you truly care about your mate, children and friends, then you will be *motivated*, or have the *energy* necessary to understand and nurture these people. In terms of experience, this simply means that *motivation provides the energy to work for a particular purpose.*

On the other hand, if you just *feel* that you care; perhaps based on shallow sentiments, noble intentions, or a sense of obligation, you will experience *conflict* between the *feeling* that you care, and the *fact* that you are not *motivated* (lack the energy) to understand and nurture your mate, children, and friends.

As a learning exercise, think about your daily priorities and determine what you most *care about*, or what *motivates* your daily priorities, choices and behaviors? For instance, are you *internally* or *externally* motivated? Do your *needs* take precedence over *wants*, or vice versa? Can you even differentiate between needs and wants? Are your intentions, needs, wants, purposes, choices and behaviors usually *congruent*, or frequently *contradictory*?

You may find it is difficult to answer these questions, perhaps because it has **not** been your habit to consciously observe, think about, and learn from everyday experience. Most people, if they think about life or themselves at all, do so in an imaginary world where they focus on how they *feel* and what they *want*, and either fail to observe, or just do not care about understanding what is true and needed.

Rather than caring about truth and needs, most of us are motivated by wanting to feel in control. Control what, you ask? Everything! To begin, we want to control our feelings, and this includes feeling financially safe in the *external* world, and emotionally safe in our *internal* world. We also want to control pleasure and pain, every relationship, and above all, we want to control feeling good about ourselves. In normal life, we are *motivated* by a desire to control.

The only problem with normal motivation is that life does ***not*** *offer control!* When we pursue something life does not offer, it means we are doomed to frustration and emptiness. It also means that we can never build internal happiness. What does life offer? For one, life offers the opportunity to *observe, think, and learn.* This means that life offers the opportunity to become conscious by observing the facts of actual experience, think about what they mean, and learn how to master our needs and potentials.

If we *observe* that everyone; rich and poor, smart and stupid, lucky and tragic, are all equipped with a mind, emotions, and body, and all are subject to illness and aging and limited by a lifespan, then we see for ourselves that at best we have only a small influence in life, never control.

Next, if we look at what creates *meaning*, we soon see that considering how quickly life passes the only thing that creates real meaning are those *internal developments* and *external experiences* that ***retain their value, over time.*** The principle of life here is that for anything in human existence to be truly meaningful, it must have ***enduring value.***

If we pause, and look again at John Muir, Anne Frank, and Emily Dickinson, we see that each one cared about and was truly *motivated* by internal developments and external experiences that had enduring value. John Muir was motivated to observe, experience, and learn about Nature. Eventually, he wanted to *understand and protect* Nature. Every step in the process had enduring value for himself, and ultimately, for all of us.

Anne Frank was motivated to explore the experience of being a young woman in an extraordinary and tragic situation. She observed, thought, and learned from every aspect of being confined in a small space with family and strangers. She wrote down her observations and thoughts so anyone reading her story can be touched, taught, and changed by a 14 year old girl who was profoundly innocent, scrupulously honest, and courageously insightful.

Emily Dickinson wanted the freedom to live and learn in her own way, in her own space, unimpeded by the prejudice and superstition of her times (I can identify quite well). Emily understood the English Language like few minds ever understand it, and took liberties with language and used it masterfully to express her very original view of all the "little" things in life.

Like most original people who see themselves accurately, Emily was at times humble, and at times innocently arrogant, but always courageous in pursuing truth, hopelessly in love with beauty, and like John and Anne was eventually rewarded with love, wisdom, and meaning (enduring value) because she was ***motivated*** by a ***desire to understand.***

It's time to look in the mirror and ask, "Well damn, what in tarnation does motivate me?" If you are normal, then you want to "enjoy life." The highest aspiration of most people, just ask them, is to *enjoy* their jobs, mates, children, and lives. Usually, the ultimate praise we can apply to any experience or accomplishment is to say how much we *enjoyed* it, or the ubiquitous, "Gosh, I just had so much *fun*!"

When someone is motivated by *wanting to enjoy,* or *have fun*, what is the consequence? Can he/she experience meaning? Well, who knows, but let's compare and contrast the *normal* experience of being motivated to enjoy, or have fun, with a *conscious* experience of being motivated by a whole-hearted desire to understand, and see what we discover.

John, Anne, and Emily were all *motivated* by a *desire to understand* themselves, life, and other people. All three lead intense lives filled with passion and insight, and all three fulfilled some or all of their internal potentials. All three whole-heartedly loved truth, beauty, and being creative. All three left an observable legacy of enduring value, which means that all three lives were undeniably "meaningful."

Now, let's compare the motivations of these "B" level famous people with normal motivations that you can see in yourself or other people.

By the way, a life is defined as *normal* when someone is *motivated* by the same things everyone else is. So anyone who wants to control pain and pleasure, security, self-image, and desires money and success is blessed with *normal* motivations, which means that a primary priority will be to *enjoy* life and have as much *fun* as possible.

Let me say here, for the record, there is absolutely nothing "wrong" with wanting to enjoy life and have fun! However, there are consequences for making enjoyment our *primary motivator.* One of the consequences is that no one with this desire as a primary motivation has ever mastered love or wisdom. The reason is that love and wisdom require being motivated by a *desire to understand,* not have fun.

No one needs to take my word for this statement. Instead, just read biographies of famous people, then observe people in the news and all the people in your personal acquaintance, and after you define both *love* and *wisdom* in terms of experience, observe who seems to have mastered one or both potentials, and note their *primary* motivation.

The paradox here is that people who become loving and wise do in fact "enjoy" life the most! What is paradoxical is that while loving and wise people enjoy life the most, *enjoyment* is never their primary motivator, *understanding* is.

Not surprisingly, out of motivation is born every priority and purpose. Motivations, priorities, and purposes are inseparably linked. Together, all three reveal far more about our lives and characters than we usually want to see, and certainly more than we want anyone else to observe! In spite of this normal reluctance, we will next define the core of everyone's identity, life, and character, those often invisible purposes that create our everyday priorities.

Purposes

Everyone's purposes are defined by his/her goals in life. With a *normal identity,* our primary purpose is to acquire control over approval, success, security, and making life enjoyable. With a *conscious identity,* our first purpose is to become loving and wise.

To confirm that the primary purpose of most people is to acquire control, simply observe yourself and other people and note that almost everyone *believes* that *happiness* is a consequence of controlling approval, success, security, and of course, having fun. While most people also *believe* that love and wisdom are valuable ideals, very few take even one consciously defined step toward achieving these internal goals.

Ironically, even though people often believe in the value of love and wisdom, they still lack a detailed process for how to achieve these goals. If you asked, "What is more important in life, making a lot of money or becoming loving and wise?" How would you answer this question? How do you suppose the imaginary *man in the street* would answer this question? My money is on most people saying they *believe* that becoming loving and wise is more important than making money!

Of course, in this jaded age I could be dead wrong. In spite of the fact that many people *believe* in love and wisdom, we can see the training most offered in normal life is how to make money in the pursuit of security and success, *not* how to become loving and wise. This normal value is supported by two powerful persuaders—advertising and self-help—and both encourage us to *get everything we want*, not pursue internal development.

In our heart of hearts, most of us believe in the power of money, success, security and approval to make us happy. On the other hand, since we see it so seldom and understand it so little, few of us *believe* in the power of love and wisdom to make us happy. Consequently, we have still not devised commonly available training programs in how to become loving and wise.

Perhaps, it's time to observe people who have been successful in pursuing normal purposes; i.e., acquired control over money, success, and fun—and note the consequences. Do the successful people you observe seem to be consciously connected to experience, internally fulfilled, whole-hearted, and competent to nurture themselves and other people? Or do the "successful" people you observe seem to be constantly busy, often disconnected from experience, and frequently trying to fill-up, but never full?

By contrast, if you see that a satisfying life is the result of acknowledging body, mind and emotions so you can feed and fulfill every real need and potential—then you will see there is in fact a *conscious process* necessary to become loving and wise. When you master this process your life will become meaningful, and you will experience real and lasting internal happiness.

When you see this conscious process acted out by someone in ordinary life, then you will know the source for the old cliché *money can't buy happiness*. You will also see how this cliché is both accurate and inaccurate. On the one hand, we all need money for material needs, and on the other, we need *mental and emotional development* to create lasting value and internal happiness.

Bottom line, we need both money and development. It is easier, however, to earn enough money to feed our *external* needs than to acquire the *internal* development necessary to become loving and wise. Also, anyone can be happy with a small amount of money, but no one can be happy with a small amount of internal development! This is why it is so important to make our *primary purpose* in life ***a whole-hearted desire to become loving and wise.***

Internal Needs

Once you understand motivations and purposes, it is time to understand *needs.* Where to start? No place like the beginning. In this case, we begin with the fact that you have ***a body, mind, emotions, and life span.*** As we have noted, these four facts set the conditions for everyone's existence. Did you ever consciously observe that as a result of having a mind, emotions, and body; you also have *mental, emotional, and physical needs and potentials* that you must *master* if you want to build internal happiness?

While everyone recognizes physical needs, we normally fail to notice that our minds and emotions have needs and potentials too. This is one reason we rarely create a *conscious purpose* to master feeding our minds truth or our emotions beauty. When we fail to feed our minds truth, we also fail to fulfill our internal potential to *understand* ourselves, life, and other people. Of course, if we fail to feed our emotions beauty, we rarely have the energy or desire to fulfill our potential to be loving and wise.

Animals have minds, emotions, bodies, and life spans too, but they are programmed by instinct to feed their needs. Dolphins, for instance, experience an emotional need to be social and are often seen to be delightfully playful with one another. People too, have an emotional need to experience social contact that is conscious, warm, playful, and caring.

People, however, seem to have more trouble feeding this internal need than Dolphins. How can that be? Well, we don't define *internal needs* and separate them from *wants*. As a result, we fail to understand internal needs, including the universal human need to be *acknowledged, understood and touched*.

Rather than make it a *conscious purpose* to feed our *need* to be acknowledged in a warm and caring atmosphere—we often pursue a *desire* for approval. We also use social situations to gratify a manipulative *desire* to *network for advantage,* or to just hang-out in proximity with other people, while we fail to either define or feed our *need* for intimacy.

By contrast, Dolphins easily separate play from survival, and are competent to feed both internal and external needs. It helps that Dolphins do not have fragile egos or self-images to support, and are never burdened by the feelings of superiority or inferiority that so often distract people away from understanding and feeding their real needs.

On average, it seems to even a casual observer that Dolphins are more masterful than humans at feeding all their needs, and in the main seem happier than most people. One thing we can learn from comparing ourselves to Dolphins is that we will never be *instinctually* happy, but instead, must teach ourselves to *understand* and *care about* both internal and external needs. Then, we must *master f*eeding every need until we create the spontaneous joy in being alive that we see expressed in the behavior and demeanor of an ordinary Bottlenose Dolphin.

To master needs, we must first learn how to *observe, think, and learn* until we can extract insight from experience. Learning from experience is required if we want to both see and define internal needs. Now, ask yourself, "Has it been my *purpose* to observe, think, and learn from everyday life?" And, "If so, have I used the insight I acquired to understand, feed, and fulfill every significant need and potential?"

As powerful as understanding is, it is impotent without the energy from *whole-hearted caring*. This means everyone must create a *conscious purpose* to develop their caring. ***If you consciously commit to these two purposes—to develop your understanding and caring—then no matter what else you may do, you will create a greater degree of happiness than you could ever achieve pursuing a normal purpose.***

After adopting a purpose to develop both consciousness and caring, the next step is to acknowledge that you are the proud owner of a remarkably durable, and at the same time, amazingly fragile human body. The meaning of this paradoxical fact is that building internal happiness requires in part, that you adopt a *purpose* to master your physical needs.

Given the availability of nutritious food and information about diet and exercise, mastering physical needs should not be the difficult task it has become here in the United States of Overweight America! Ironically, if we were more competent at feeding our *internal* mental and emotional needs, it would be much easier to master our *external* physical needs.

When people are hungry for *internal* experiences they cannot define, the chronic frustration they routinely experience is often acted out by trying to fill-up *externally*. This is one reason we Americans do almost everything too much. We eat too much, work too much, entertain too much, medicate too much, and are way too obsessed with trying to be important or rich rather than happy. What's wrong with this picture?

The biggest flaw in this picture is that normal American purposes are not in harmony with internal needs. In our lust to acquire and control, we frequently fail to master our most basic physical need for a well-conditioned and healthy body.

It is important to see that normal purposes are based on what we want, while conscious purposes are created to feed what we need. The most basic requirement for becoming wise is to teach yourself how to *want what you need.* This means that if you want to be wise, learn how to love yourself, and eventually become competent to build internal happiness, then you must adopt a *conscious purpose* to master every significant need and potential—internal and external.

Choices and Behaviors

Nothing so illuminates our contradictions quite as easily as contrasting motivations, purposes and needs—with choices and behaviors. For instance, we may believe we truly love our mates, family, and friends; that is, until we actually observe our choices and behaviors and see that in fact we have not committed the energy and effort necessary to understand and nurture these people. A lack of both commitment and mastery reveals a *contradiction* between our *purpose* (to love mate, family, and friends) and our *behavior* (failure to become competent at nurturing them internally and externally).

Another example occurs when we believe we *love* living but never master our needs and potentials—internal and external. When we fail to master our needs and potentials, we reveal a lack of *caring* about ourselves and life that contradicts the *belief* that we *love* living. Please note that one critical source of unhappiness is creating contradictions that we fail to observe, understand, and resolve.

Understanding ourselves, other people, human history, or even large institutions like governments, educational systems, or entire cultures can be accomplished in part by first identifying the person or system's motivations, purposes, and needs—and then observing the degree of congruence or contradiction that exists with its priorities, choices and behaviors.

An easy to observe principle of life is that the more contradictory a person, institution, or culture becomes; the more ineffective, divided, corrupt and unhappy it will be.

The opposite is also true; the more a person, institution, or culture's motivations, purposes, and needs are *congruent* with its choices and behaviors, the more he/she/it will create integrity, competence, and enduring happiness.

Building a Conscious Identity

In the last two chapters, you have acquired enough information to ask and answer the question, "Who am I?" The layers of detail in your answers will define your *identity.* Unless like John Muir, Anne Frank, and Emily Dickinson, you were born with an innate *desire* to understand life and taught yourself how to *observe, think, and learn*, then no matter what you may believe, you may discover that you have developed a *normal* identity with certain predictable characteristics.

To an untrained eye people appear unique, or special, and in some external ways this is true. On the other hand, we are all trainable nervous systems and become products of our parents, times, and training. When our training is normal, our parents, teachers, and culture ignore the *meaning* of the four basic facts—mind, emotions, body, and lifespan—and never clearly define internal needs and potentials.

In addition, in normal life we are rarely if ever taught how to fulfill our internal potential to *understand, care, master, create, and contribute*, so we have no process for building internal development into our response to being alive. This means we also fail to learn how to feed *internal needs* and never develop the skills necessary to *think for understanding and build bonded relationships.*

The consequence is that most of us are saddled not only with a *normal*, but also to some degree a *neurotic* identity (*neurotic* simply means anxious, conflicted, or contradictory). With a normal and to some degree neurotic identity, we are largely unaware that *internal needs and potentials* even exist, and as a result, rarely define or master a single one. Our *purposes a*re also largely unconscious and normal, which as we have seen, means that we value security, success, approval and entertainment. Sadly, mild variations in degree or emphasis in these basic themes will not take us out of being trapped by a normal identity.

Rather than develop a *burning desire to understand*, a normal identity develops a mind that prefers certainty, so we often like to rigidly adhere to our opinions and judgments—remarkably—even about issues or topics we know we have never consciously thought about or explored! We can test for a normal identity by asking, "Do I consciously listen?" Then, "Do I purposefully ask intelligent questions and allow myself to be changed by the answers?" Or, "Do I tend to have answers for most issues, and if I am quiet it is primarily to be polite, so the sad result is that I am rarely changed by someone else's thought?"

With normal training, we are not taught how to define even our own perspective. One consequence is that we cannot become competent to feed needs and fulfill potentials or build emotional bonds, and both love and wisdom remain vague and undefined ideals that we hope will happen as a result of aging, but have no plan for actually attaining.

The identity we develop, normal or conscious, determines how we respond to the sometimes inspiring and sometimes overwhelming mystery of just being alive. With a normal identity, we replace innocence with manipulation, and curiosity with answers, and our primary response to being alive is to pursue control. A normal identity develops a purpose to control life that discourages all attempts to acquire understanding, which explains how human beings can have been around for so long and yet have made so little progress in our collective ability to become loving and wise. ***A normal identity simply does not support the development of love and wisdom.***

Fulfilling our human potential to master love and wisdom requires that we actively and purposefully build a *conscious identity* based on being innocently curious and backed-up by a *desire to understand*. A *conscious purpose* to master observing, thinking, and learning so we acquire the insight necessary to build genuine wisdom is the foundation for all internal development.

This book provides a detailed step by step *process* for internal development that anyone can use to improve his/her everyday life and create a greater degree of internal fulfillment. If you want to work to the top of this developmental staircase, you will become loving and wise. This is life at its fullest, no matter what your external circumstances may be, positive or negative. When you can live *internal* life at its fullest, no matter what the *external* circumstances, then like John, Anne, and Emily, your existence will be rich with satisfaction and you will be rewarded with enduring value—a meaningful life!

Understanding Love, Wisdom & Identity

Many people believe they have already become loving and wise, or at worst, they will develop these internal qualities as a result of aging and experience. Just for fun, observe the people around you; perhaps people in the news, journalists, politicians, educators, priests and ministers, as well as family and your circle of friends and acquaintances. How many people do you see qualify as genuinely loving and wise?

Even more importantly, can you define love and wisdom in terms of concrete and observable facts well-enough to discriminate between someone who is truly loving and wise, and someone who is not? You may be the exception, but in over thirty years of talking to people about their issues, I have never met anyone who has even tried to think about love and wisdom in enough concrete and observable detail to actually define both words in *experiential*—not conceptual—terms.

Many people over the years have "felt" they understood love and wisdom, but no one I have met consciously created clear definitions and then used those definitions to master the required skills and awareness. Throughout this book, I offer detailed definitions and specific skills necessary to express love, as well as occasional *principles of life* that represent *bits of wisdom.* For now, however, let's see if we can define the *experience* of love and wisdom. Then we will see how love and wisdom fit with the development of identity—both normal and conscious.

Defining Love & Wisdom

What does the experience of love look like? Well, John, Anne, and Emily all loved truth, beauty, and life. How do we know? All three *consciously pursued understanding in spite of pain, obstacles, and loneliness*. In addition, all three fed their basic internal needs and created a *conscious* identity that was original and authentic, and all three were deeply committed to their purposes.

If we observe John, Anne, and Emily and identify the qualities that express love, we first see that we *need* to be committed just to begin, and then we must be willing to *work and suffer* until we can *understand and nurture* what we love; no matter how much criticism, aloneness, anonymity, or ridicule we encounter.

If we also want to love both truth and beauty, then like John, Anne & Emily, we need to *commit* to *working and suffering* until we are *internally competent* to pursue truth and experience beauty. By definition, if we want to love a person then we need to *work* until we *understand* internal and external needs, and then actually *nurture* the other person. If we want to *love* wisdom, we need to *commit* our time and energy to *master* observing, thinking, and learning until we see the critical patterns that define in detail the *universal* issues, needs, and potentials that apply to ourselves, as well as every other human being.

Is this how you would have defined love? If not, how would you define love? Is your definition precise and based on *facts* so you can define specific skills, or is it so vague and *feeling* based there are no skills to learn, or actions to take?

In defining love, we also identified the *process* necessary to develop wisdom—that is, we must *master observing, thinking, and learning until we see the critical patterns that define the universal issues, needs, and potentials that affect all human beings*. Just as with love, becoming wise requires that we embody the internal qualities of commitment, work, suffering, and understanding. Please note there is nothing in these definitions about how you *feel* or what you *believe*. Instead, it is all about what you understand and become internally competent to provide.

Conscious vs. Normal Identity

In the two previous chapters we began to define *identity* by asking the question, "Who am I?" At first, we observed that everyone is a *trained nervous system* that has already reacted to the four facts. Then, we asked "who am I" based on internal potentials and learned even more about ourselves.

Finally, we identified the five elements that define each person's *perspective* so we could see our internal life in more detail. Viewing internal development from multiple angles will help to create a mental picture of our identity.

We can use the metaphor of building a house to understand how identities are built. In normal life, acquiring control is the primary purpose, which forms the *foundation* of a normal *identity*. Building on the *foundation* of wanting *control,* we then construct the walls of a normal identity by pursuing *security, image, success, and entertainment.* The roof of a normal identity is the desire to experience *planned oblivion.*

It is important to see that "identity" simply refers to what we *identify with*, not necessarily *who we are*. Over a lifetime, however, what we identify with and who we are merge, and eventually become one. As we have seen, the primary problem of a normal identity is that it will not support love and wisdom.

Mastering love and wisdom require we build a *conscious* identity on the solid *foundation* of *understanding and caring*—not trying to acquire the illusion of control. Then, we need to build the walls of our *conscious* identity on *mastery, creativity, and contribution*. The solid support provided by fulfilling these internal potentials is necessary to add *love and wisdom*—the roof of a *conscious identity.*

It is critical to see that love and wisdom require a conscious identity built step by step on the foundation created by fulfilling potentials. It is also essential to observe that it is impossible to develop love and wisdom on the foundation of trying to acquire control. When you imagine a *normal identity* based on wanting *control* versus a *conscious identity* based on a *desire* to *understand and nurture*, which one seems to best represent what you identify with, and have actually integrated on a daily basis?

The answer to this question defines who you are now, which leads to the critical question, "*Who do you want to be*?" When you understand both normal and conscious identities, you can answer this question, and for the first time, you have options! In the past, people have not had any real options because religion, spiritual pursuits, and philosophy have offered ideas and beliefs but no objective, clearly defined, or concrete path on how to become loving and wise.

It is important to see that internal happiness is a collateral benefit of becoming loving and wise. Happiness, love, and wisdom are all a consequence of internal development, which can be defined in part as acquiring a *complex sequence of skills and awareness*. ***To become loving and wise requires we develop our minds and emotions by building a conscious identity based on mastering internal needs and potentials. Internal happiness is one consequence of this development.***

Self-Awareness vs. Self-Absorption

One difference between normal and conscious identities—and the source of observable changes in our motivations and purposes—can be seen when we shift away from normal *self-absorption* to being *consciously and competently self-aware*. So you ask, "Exactly, what is the difference?"

First, a normally trained mind is constantly *absorbed* in its own beliefs, feelings, prejudices, obsessions and fantasies. This means that with a normal identity we do not even try to master observing, thinking, and learning, but instead spend our life's time obsessing, feeling, and fantasizing. With a normal identity, we rarely develop the desire, nor are we trained in how to build a *conscious awareness* of ourselves, other people, or life.

You can verify this statement by noting how little people seem to understand either themselves, or life! In fact, it is rare for someone to show whole-hearted interest in learning about himself, life, or other people. Instead, most people's minds are richly stocked with answers, opinions, and judgments—but pitifully poor in accurate observations and intelligent questions.

John, Anne, and Emily are examples of people who wanted to accurately observe themselves, life and other people. They used ordinary observations to *understand* themselves, not *obsess* about themselves. They also wanted to experience life, and as a result, quickly learned that self-absorbed fantasizing got in the way of experiencing, observing and understanding, which made self-absorption a waste of time, energy and life. In stark contrast, for a mind with normal training, obsessing and fantasizing but never understanding is not only acceptable, it is expected!

When we work to become *self-aware,* we want to understand every real need and potential, and then become competent to feed and fulfill both. In developing self-awareness, we eventually come to understand ourselves, which in turn, creates the internal freedom to focus on understanding life and other people. In sad contrast, a normal mind is never fulfilled, and as a result is inevitably condemned to a lifetime of frustrating and futile self-absorption where satisfaction and meaning are forever out of its developmental reach.

Like in a Greek tragedy, normal identities are sentenced to forever search, but never find. Conscious identities, however, observe, think, and learn until they become loving, wise, and internally happy.

The Internal Potential For Real *Caring*

The two potentials that set human beings apart from other animals are the ability to *understand* complex realities, and the ability to develop whole-hearted *caring*. In the last three chapters we defined the beginning steps necessary to fulfill the human potential for understanding, and now, we will explore the other critical human potential, the ability to *care* whole-heartedly. The purpose in this chapter is to *understand* the experience of caring, not define in detail how to create and express it. That will come later in **Part II**, when we first define and then learn how to feed internal needs.

Source of Caring

Take a moment and try to define what you care about. Perhaps you care about your mate, child, friends or extended family? Or maybe you care about nature, accumulating knowledge, competing, or some material thing like your car, home, stereo, etc. Once you identify the objects or activities you care about, think again to see if you can identify the ***source*** of the caring itself.

Perhaps surprisingly, you may discover that *hunger* is the source of the emotional energy we refer to as *caring*. By hunger, I mean whatever you need, want, long for, or simply hope will provide security, survival, pleasure, self-worth, satisfaction or meaning. If you doubt that hunger is the source of caring, then try to imagine *caring* about something when you feel no desire, need, or hunger.

You may find that without the experience of hunger you feel no energy, and when there is no energy—there is no caring.

Normally, we are unaware of the source of our caring. This is one reason that romantic love seems so mysterious; that is, the source of our experience is often invisible. Nonetheless, if we want to *understand* the experience of love, we must identify the hungers and anticipated satisfactions that together are the *source* of the intense energy we call caring, or love.

If people defined internal needs they would soon see the *sources* of real caring. Unfortunately, we rarely identify and define internal needs. Instead, the *experience* of caring is often a mystery, in part, because we are unaware of our internal hungers and explain caring in terms of lofty *concepts* rather than as an *emotional response* to our internal and external needs and wants.

The need for self-worth is one example of an internal need that generates energy. Most people believe that approval creates self-worth, and as a result, *care* about approval. Sometimes, our desire to feel good about ourselves is so great we will do almost anything to get approval. The only problem is that approval is a judgment that feels pleasant for a moment and gratifies our *desire* to feel special, but fails to feed our *need* for understanding, and so, leaves us empty inside rather than fulfilled.

A similar process occurs with almost every other need and want, both internal and external. As we have seen, we *need* to eat food that provides energy and health, but we *want* to eat for pleasure and comfort. In gratifying our desire for pleasure and comfort, we *want* food rich in sugar and fat even though we *need* nutritious food that creates energy and health.

When we experience conflict between an *external* need and want, like the need for nutritious food vs. a desire to eat for pleasure or comfort, we often recognize there is a problem even if we do nothing to resolve it. However, when we experience conflict between *internal* needs and wants, we rarely even notice there is a problem, which is one reason we often fail to *care* about internal needs.

One example of this process can be seen in that most people *want* a mate to fill up their internal emptiness and make them feel happy.

On the other hand, everyone *needs* a mate he/she can share and grow with, as well as give to. This means we *need* to care about *growing* in consciousness and caring so we can *share* reality, purposes, and quintessential moments. With normal training, however, we *want* to get security, approval or passion, and fail to understand our *need* to grow, give, and share.

A similar conflict occurs in defining a purpose for living. Almost everyone *wants* external success so he can feel secure and create a comfortable and pleasant life. Many people are even quite successful in gratifying these desires. The only problem is we *need* to master growing, giving, and sharing. When we create a life of security and pleasantness but fail to develop internally, then instead of becoming happy we just feel bored, emotionally isolated, and empty.

Whether in relationships, or our individual lives, when we value *wants* over *needs* we lose all hope for internal happiness. The challenge is to *understand* wants and needs, and then *care about* and choose to master our needs. One way to create the motivation to care about needs is to observe experience until we understand that ignoring our needs in order to gratify wants will create emptiness and frustration—not internal happiness.

Real vs. Neurotic Caring

Caring generated by feeding real needs is genuine. So when parents feed a child's internal needs, he/she feels satisfied and safe, and over time, loved. One consequence is that through the experience of being loved the child learns to care about himself, life, and other people. This is why children of caring parents learn how to care, while children of abusive parents tend to become abusive. The pattern here is that children normally imitate and repeat what they have experienced.

It is important to note that adults too tend to imitate and repeat their significant experiences rather than learn from them. If people were taught to *learn from experience* rather than unconsciously repeat it, then children of both loving and abusive parents would grow up caring and compassionate.

The presence of real caring is determined in part by a person's *commitment* to give as much time, effort, and energy as someone or something actually needs. Another indication our caring is real is that we become *internally competent to* understand and nurture. This means that if we genuinely care about a child or mate then we become competent to acknowledge, understand, and nurture our child or mate, internally and externally. By the same token, if we truly care about ourselves, then we master every need and potential.

By contrast, normal neurotic or *imaginary* caring can be observed when someone *believes* he/she cares about a child or mate but fails to devote time, effort, and energy, and as a result, never becomes competent to understand and nurture. Or someone claims to care about his own life, but remains forever inadequate to feed and fulfill his needs and potentials.

Neurotic caring comes in two forms. One, we just pretend to care, in part so we can look like a good person. In this case, we project the image that we care for the purpose of getting approval. The other form of neurotic caring occurs when we ignore needs and gratify desires and experience a degree of pleasure, but no real satisfaction. Then, in spite of being frustrated, we persist in pursuing every desire with nary an observation or question about what is needed.

Repeating behaviors that we know from experience are unsatisfying creates anxiety and depression. Unfortunately, the belief that *gratifying wants should create happiness* is a normal assumption that few people ever seriously question. What makes this assumption neurotic is that we rigidly continue to believe that gratifying desires will make us happy in spite of overwhelming experience proving the opposite. One consequence is that in pursuing our belief that gratifying desires *should* make us happy, we become chronically discontent, anxious, or internally divided, i.e. neurotic.

The Signs of Real Caring

It's time to acknowledge that *congruent actions* rather than words, intentions, beliefs, or feelings show that *real caring* is present. In normal life, we create confusion when we define caring in terms of feelings or intentions, rather than the fact of feeding needs. Nothing is more disappointing than when our mate or parent offers silly sentiments or grandiose intentions **not** backed-up by genuine energy, effort, and the competence to feed real needs.

The signs of real caring are easily observed. That is, we *commit* the required energy and effort necessary to actually grow in our ability to *understand and nurture.* In romantic relationships, real caring is expressed in part by acknowledging our mate's perspective. In the process of learning about our mate, we identify her motivations and purposes and nurture her needs. If we do not become competent to feed our mate's needs, then our caring is more about creating an image, or pretending that we care, than in actually loving her.

To test this observation, observe yourself in relationship with your mate, friends, or children and note whether you *believe* you care about these people. Next, notice whether or not you are competent to feed your own internal needs, as well as those of another person. Can you even define an internal need? If you take credit for caring when you are unable to feed internal needs, then you create *conflict* between the *feeling* you care and the *fact* that you are not competent to understand and nurture. This conflict creates a contradiction that will be frustrating for you, and damaging to the people close to you.

When you commit time, effort, and attention to defining internal and external needs—and become competent to feed them—then your caring will be useful and real.

On the other hand, if you feel sentimental, but your feelings are not supported by a commitment of time, energy, and effort, as well as the ability to nurture, then your caring is mostly a superficial façade or fanciful image that is not backed-up by the facts of your actions.

When Caring Becomes Love

Any distinction between caring and love must be to a degree subjective and arbitrary. I offer a distinction here to identify levels, or degrees of the same experience. Predictably, *love* is built with the same skills and awareness that create *caring*. This means that committing energy and effort to first understand and then nurture ourselves and other people are basic requirements for both caring and love.

In addition to these basic requirements, for me, caring becomes love when the commitment becomes *permanent,* and is not altered or lost due to changes in circumstances, proximity, or suffering. In normal life, love, at least as many people seem to define it, is often distressingly fragile and easily modified or destroyed by the most trivial of events.

You may have experienced friendships or a romantic relationship that seemed solid but then died due to trivial changes in circumstances, perceived benefit, or proximity. Perhaps the relationship required a degree of effort, or suffering, or maybe it was just no longer convenient. In any case, when relationships die from trivial causes, or just fade away, it is clear they were not built on sharing and caring, and certainly, not on love.

Of course, the relationship where love is most needed is in building emotional bonds between parents and children. Sadly, this relationship so critical to everyone's development is easily plagued by conflicts, criticism, or indifference. Even when family conflicts are not openly acknowledged, the underlying reality is often an *absence* of real caring, and the *presence* of a superficial friendliness that we frequently call *love,* but is in fact only a façade, an emotionally empty form, or a feeling of obligation.

To transform caring into a permanent bond that qualifies as* love *requires mental and emotional development. Internal development begins with understanding our own perspective; and then expands into understanding the perspectives of our mate, friends, and family members. Next, we must continue to grow until our internal commitment to understand and nurture

changes from temporary to permanent, and is no longer subject to change.

Take a moment and ask whether you understand your own *motivations, purposes, needs, wants, choices and behaviors*—consciously, and in detail? Do you understand anyone else's perspective? Do you *love* your own life? Do you truly *love* another person? Can you imagine how you would respond if someone fed your need to be understood and nurtured, and cared about your internal needs as much as his own? Do you think you might experience some degree of being loved?

The Internal Potential For ***Mastery***

People are happiest when they are *building* or *mastering*. To test this statement, just ask, "When was I the happiest?" Perhaps it was when you were *building* a career, home and family, or in the process of becoming educated, *mastering* a sport or musical instrument, or consciously engaged in any activity where you acquire layer upon layer of awareness and skill.

The experience of challenging your mind, emotions, and body while working toward a life-affirming goal is a reliable source of enduring satisfaction. If one of your goals is to become loving and wise, then the satisfaction you experience from fulfilling this goal will be *permanent*, which is also a definition for truly *meaningful.*

Making Mastery a "Conscious" Purpose

Historically, people have always believed that happiness is a function of acquiring power or pleasure. Both theologians and philosophers have agreed that man's basic character, or "human nature" is defined by a limitless lust for power and pleasure. Religion and philosophy have also agreed that man's unruly and greedy impulses are incorrigible and must be controlled for civilization to exist and prosper.

Where religion and philosophy have disagreed is on how to respond to man's character flaws. Religion has advocated *believing* in a living god who is always watching and cares whether or not we do the "right" thing. What is *right* is defined by each culture, usually in terms of its current perception of its best interest or external advantage. The carrot that religion offers for following its rules of conduct, besides god's approval, is the promise of a pleasant immortality. The stick or punishment for not following the rules is still immortality, but it is an excruciatingly painful eternity!

Even though the particulars vary, most religions offer some variation on this theme, and the purpose is the same. That is, the purpose of religion is to create internal controls, so people will behave in ways we have come to believe are civilized, right, lawful, and cooperative.

Philosophy agrees with religion that controlling human nature is necessary, but instead of *beliefs* offers *ideas* about how we should structure politics and invent morals to create a cooperative society. In Western Civilization, Aristotle and Plato set the stage for all subsequent thought. Aristotle was the quintessential conservative, and Plato offered an eclectic mix of liberal and conservative ideas and proposals.

Aristotle thought that an aristocracy was needed to rule the masses, which he believed were by nature primitive and more than a bit brutish. By contrast, Plato proposed an authoritarian meritocracy that would select people in terms of intelligence and talent, and then train them for positions in society where their strengths would be best employed.

The point is that both philosophy and religion agree with the assumption that people have a basically fearful and greedy "human nature" that must be controlled. ***I am challenging this historical assumption with the hypothesis that just maybe what we have assumed to be built into our collective and genetic character is in fact mostly a consequence of environment and training, and so, can be changed.***

For instance, people have always believed that the main sources of happiness are power and pleasure. They have also assumed that more power or pleasure creates more happiness. Most civilizations have embraced these *beliefs* as *fact*, and then passed them from generation to generation. One consequence of accepting these beliefs as facts is that people compete for the scarce resources of power and pleasure. This competition makes people relentless adversaries.

Since power and pleasure gratify wants not needs, no one can ever get enough to be happy. One consequence is that in pursuing power and pleasure, feelings of fear and greed are infinitely renewed. To this extent, both religion and philosophy have been accurate in their sad diagnosis. **However, *what if happiness is a consequence of mastering our needs and potentials and becoming loving and wise?***

If we test this hypothesis by educating people in how to *master* their needs and potentials—and if each person becomes a little more conscious and caring and experiences some degree of internal happiness—then maybe we can add a new quality to "human nature." This new quality will be the new human nature, which will be inherently *cooperative* rather than instinctually *adversarial.* What do you think; is it worth checking out?

To test the hypothesis that mastering needs and potentials and becoming loving and wise will create happiness, try making *mastery* a *conscious purpose.* This requires making it your priority to master understanding and caring, as well as every other need and potential. ***Mastery does not require perfection; it only requires that you become skillful, and internally competent enough to create satisfaction and meaning.***

Mastery is a building block of enduring human happiness. For instance, if you learn how to play a musical instrument, or just become a competent listener, you will experience satisfaction. This process applies to every life-affirming activity. So, whether you want to be a chef, gardener, musician, homemaker, bread-winner, or snake charmer, each arena of mastery will increase your degree of satisfaction.

Mastering Understanding

Understanding is a consequence learning how to observe, think, and learn. Below is a handy four-step formula to help you observe and think about any issue, topic, or need.

Formula to Explore for Understanding

- ***Identify*** a significant topic.
- ***Observe*** the topic in detail.
- ***Explore*** the topic—ask questions and think until you create layers of insight.
- ***Discover*** what is true—learn from the facts and allow them to teach and change you.

There are two keys to making this formula work for you. The first is learning how to *select* a meaningful topic, and the second is learning how to *explore* a topic by making accurate observations and asking intelligent questions. Just for fun, let's go through an example and see how the formula works.

Selecting a meaningful topic may be more difficult than you might imagine. Any topic that defines a real need, internal or external, is always a meaningful choice. Also, any topic that you truly care about is significant. One universally significant topic is defined by the question, "How do I create a genuine emotional bond with my mate, child, or friend?"

To explore this question, we must begin by defining the critical words, so we must ask, "*What is a genuine emotional bond?*" Definitions are hard, so people avoid thinking about them. How does the following definition fit with your experience?

An emotional bond is a consequence of growing, giving, and sharing together. This means we need to grow in our understanding and share reality, purposes, and quintessential moments. We must also give energy and attention, and learn how to understand each other's perspective.

Can you see that just defining a genuine emotional bond takes us a long way toward understanding how to offer one? Next, we need to further *explore* our question by asking, "*Precisely, what must I* ***do*** *to share reality, purposes, and quintessential moments?*" Finally, to truly master emotional bonding, we must understand our own and another person's motivations, needs, purposes, choices and behaviors.

Each step toward *understanding* the process of emotional bonding will add insight to our understanding. Over time, our insight will accumulate until we can define and master the skills necessary to offer and receive a genuine emotional bond. Luckily, the *process* required to both understand and master emotional bonding is the same as for understanding anything else in life.

Making it our conscious purpose to master the ability to understand ourselves, life, and other people is a reliable path to also mastering love and wisdom.

Mastering Needs

Mastery is itself a basic mental and emotional need, as well as internal potential. This only means we all *need* to grow in both external and internal competence all our lives. The day we stop mastering is the day we start dying. One sign of old age and beginning to *wait for death* is to contract mentally and emotionally. Sometimes, this process begins very early in life!

The most alive and intensely happy people will be those who pursue new challenges, acquire new awareness, and master new skills every day of their passionately lived lives. Mastering *external* skills and awareness is as important as mastering *internal* skills and awareness. Life requires both.

If you want the internal happiness that is a consequence of becoming loving and wise, then consciously commit to mastering every truly significant external and internal need. How do you determine whether or not a need is significant? That's simple: differentiate wants from needs and master every real need. If there is time left over, master wants too!

Internal Needs—Personal

It is helpful to make a list of internal needs so we can see how and where to apply the process of understanding and caring. External needs are easily defined by our need for food clothing, shelter, transportation, education and financial stability.

Internal needs are defined by our need for acknowledgment and understanding, self-worth, truth, beauty, meaningful work, and emotionally bonded relationships. We also need to fulfill our "universal" potential to become loving and wise that we share in common with all human beings, as well as every "unique" internal potential.

You can see this is a long list that can feel daunting, but you can also be encouraged that it is not likely you will run out of work before you run out of life! And exactly, what about this fact is encouraging? For one, everyone needs *meaningful work*, and developing our minds and emotions through *mastering love and wisdom* is meaningful work, which as we have noted is necessary for internal happiness.

Can you see that as you grow in mastery your choices and behaviors will change to be congruent with your needs, purposes, and potentials? Where you once looked forward to the day when you would have no more work to do—now, you feel grateful for always having more work to do! The reason for this change is observing that you need work to give your life meaning. You also need enjoyment to provide contrast, renewal, and the joy of pure playfulness.

Everyone needs both work and pleasure to be complete. People also need to be powerful. The problem is real power is created by using understanding and caring to master needs and fulfill our potential to become loving and wise. Few people in history have developed this kind of power, and those who have, failed to teach the rest of us.

Internal Needs—Relationships

People often try to create a romantic relationship before mastering their personal internal needs, and the outcome is always some degree of disappointment. The reason is simple—***a mutually satisfying and emotionally bonded relationship requires two people who can feed themselves and are internally competent to stand alone,***

share, grow, and give. With these requirements, can you see why few romantic relationships are mutually satisfying and emotionally bonded?

Did you ever think that a romantic relationship requires you to be *internally competent to stand alone*? Most people think relationships are all about being together, and in some ways this is true. The problem is that the foundation of any relationship is defined by the internal development of the two people who form it. If one or both people are internally dependent, then the purpose for being in the relationship is to "get something!"

So you blink twice, and say, "Well yeah, why else would anyone want to be in a relationship?" The assumption is that the purpose of a relationship is to get someone to feed our needs. This is the normal reason we enter a romantic relationship, and at the same time, how we create conflict and dissatisfaction. The problem is we often want a mate to feed needs that are our responsibility all alone, which means our mate cannot be successful, and we will be disappointed.

On the other hand, if two people can each stand alone—in part, because each one has mastered his internal needs, then together, they have an *abundance* of energy and understanding to offer—and *sharing and giving* become possible. ***Sharing and giving require an abundance of energy and understanding, and since most people become couples with a deficit in both, each person is frequently so hungry for attention and fulfillment that he/she has little or nothing to offer.***

Of course, when two people are in deficit mode and disappointed with each other, one solution is to have children! The hope is that children will give the purpose, attention, and internal fulfillment the couple has failed to provide for each other. This is always a futile hope. Never mind though, we would not want to give up on an ancient human hope just because it is based on fantasy and doomed to be disappointing.

What then is required to make romantic relationships *mutually satisfying and meaningful*, so both people are happy? As we have seen, step one is for each person to develop his mind and emotions until he/she can stand alone and feed real needs. Next, both people must master giving and sharing.

Give what? We need to give energy, attention, acknowledgment and understanding. The whole world is hungry for all four experiences. We first want these experiences from our parents, and when that fails, as it often does, we want our mates to provide what our parents did not. This one issue is the key to the success or failure of most relationships.

If two people learn how to give **but never expect** energy, attention, acknowledgment and understanding, then every issue can be explored and resolved. On the other hand, most couples cannot give these experiences, but desperately want to get them from their mates. As a result few if any issues are explored, while most conflicts get swept under the emotional rug to become energy draining resentments that accumulate over time.

The accumulation of unresolved issues that turn into resentments is the silent killer of many relationships. Even if a couple *stays the course,* the accumulation of resentments so often strains every interaction that disappointment, distance, or indifference becomes the dominant emotion. Not the *happily ever after* most people assume when they begin passionately in love!

In addition to giving understanding and caring, *sharing* is an absolute requirement for happy relationships. Sharing what, you may ask? Sharing a love for experiencing life is a fine place to begin. There are a million ways to experience life so it is not what or how you share, but that you passionately pursue life-affirming experiences that you *consciously* share with your mate.

If you have few or no *passionate preferences* then it will be difficult or even impossible for anyone to share with you. The reason is that you have no energy to connect with. On the other hand, if you are *judgmental* in your preferences, and belittle or demean the passions of other people, you will be just as impossible to share with or relate to. The trick is to develop preferences of your own, and also be available to expand your field of interest so you can *share* in your mate's *passionate preferences.* Of course, you will feel that you have found your one and only "soul mate" when many or most of your mate's passionate preferences mirror your own.

Internal growth is another critical need required for being happy in a romantic relationship, in part, because it is the source of newness, and newness is a source of passion. In long term relationships, renewing our passion can often be a problem. Internal development solves this problem by providing a life-affirming source of renewable energy necessary to keep all our relationships intensely alive and passionate.

One problem with this solution is that most people want to feel secure as quickly as possible in a new relationship. In the pursuit of feeling secure, they unwittingly and unintentionally destroy the source of the passion they so desperately wanted to feel. ***The issue is that people "need" a degree of life-affirming risk and uncertainty in their relationships, but they "want" to feel perfectly safe and secure.***

Once again, we must learn *to want what we need*. This is difficult when we desperately want to feel secure in our romantic relationship. In fact, we do need the security that comes from trusting our mates to be honest and responsible. Paradoxically, we also need the life-affirming risk and uncertainty that comes from knowing our mates will continue to grow on their own. ***This means we must want the responsibility to "earn our keep" by giving attention and caring while being an energy source, not an energy drain.***

Internal Needs—Profession

Now that you know something about internal *personal* and *relationship* needs, we can explore *professional* needs. One obvious fact is that our profession or job takes up the lion's share of our life's time. Since nothing is more precious than time, everyone *needs* to make his/her work *meaningful*.

Normally, people do not acknowledge just how huge a portion of their life's time is spent *on the job*. Nor do people recognize that if they want their lives to be meaningful, then work must be something they can love and learn from. If we were trained to acknowledge these facts, then we would be much more careful in our choice of work or profession.

Sadly, most people choose a job based on convenience, financial reward, image, or someone else's expectations. If you fall into one of these categories, then making your work meaningful is just a bit more challenging. So whether you love your job or not, you can make it meaningful by using everyday responsibilities to observe life, think and learn, and in the process use your work time to discover the timeless principles necessary to develop wisdom.

The Internal Potential
To be ***Creative***

The first three internal potentials—*understanding, caring, and mastery*—provide the foundation necessary to take the next step toward internal development—becoming *creative*. As a young man, I thought being *creative* was reserved for artists like Mozart, Beethoven, Michelangelo, and Shakespeare. While I still feel these men qualify as *icons of creativity*, I have expanded my definition of *creative to* include attitudes and character traits that all people need to develop if they want to build internal happiness.

In revising and expanding my definition of creativity, I observed that Mozart, Beethoven, Michelangelo, and Shakespeare all acquired *passionate preferences* they pursued with an intense degree of *consciously focused caring*. In addition, each artist worked to understand his passionate preferences, in part, by *mastering* every skill and awareness necessary to experience and express his art to the maximum allowed by his talent and lifespan.

Finally, in learning about these four icons of creativity, I saw that each one was undeniably *authentic and original*. Interestingly enough, we expect iconic humans to be authentic and original but never expect these qualities in politicians and businessmen—or ourselves! Instead, the standard for all ordinary people is to *follow the norm*, which means we pursue approval rather than authenticity, and *passively* become mediocre rather than *actively* strive to be original.

Authentic & Original

Creativity is the child of authenticity and originality. To be authentic requires that we develop a *burning desire* to experience life exactly as it is: painful, pleasant, and neutral. In being authentic, we acknowledge success and failure, gain and loss, longing and fulfillment—without ever trying to protect our feelings.

In contrast to being authentic, in normal life we learn to *manipulate* the information we allow into consciousness as we try to protect our self-image, sacred beliefs, or sentimental feelings. As a result, we often deny or distort information that we are afraid might increase our pain or responsibility. We often expect devious behavior from politicians and used car salesmen, but it can come as a shock to see that we too, frequently fail to honestly observe and consciously acknowledge our responsibility for creating painful realities.

The quintessential mate for authenticity—is originality. If you study the lives of Beethoven, Mozart, Shakespeare, or Michelangelo, you will see that each man's *originality* was built upon his *authentic* response to being alive. What lesser talents do is rely on ideas, beliefs, or feelings rather than their own direct and honest experiences and responses.

The lesson for us ordinary talents is that if we want to be creative, then we must first learn to be authentic and original. Authentic means that we need to be honest in acknowledging ourselves, life, and other people. So if we observe that our parents or mates say they care about us, but do not act caring, then we must acknowledge the facts, "I really want my parents to love me, but their actions indicate that I am rarely if ever on their minds, and their lack of questions and focused attention reveals an *absence of interest* that I cannot in all honesty, call *love.*" rather than the more normal, "I know my parents love me, they just do not know how to show it."

It requires an authentic mind to acknowledge facts that are painful, whether in acknowledging our life span, our own inadequacies, or that someone we want to love us really doesn't. How does authenticity first lead to being original, and then creative? Well, being original requires that we see everything in life accurately and do not allow our desire to avoid pain and feel good, or to fit in and belong, to dissuade us from observing and acknowledging the truth.

When we have the courage to be original, we study the past just like Beethoven, Mozart, Michelangelo, and Shakespeare studied the past, learn what people before us have said and done, and then strike out in our own *original* way to express our *unique* experiences and talents. Few people have the degree of talent that the four icons of creativity possessed, but we can all learn to be authentic and original, and then develop the degree of creativity we do possess to the full extent of our potential. Building on the foundation of becoming authentic and original, we next need to develop truly *passionate preferences* to focus our attention, direct our energy, and provide meaningful challenges to master.

Passionate Preferences

As everyone knows, the four icons of creativity were *passionate* about life and their art. Contrast this attitude with what you observe in everyday life. ***How many people do you know care about anything enough to devote their time, energy, and caring with undivided interest, whole-hearted passion, and a permanent life-time commitment?***

How about yourself, do you have things in your life that you love so completely that you can say, "Yes! I care about X with my undivided interest and whole-hearted passion, and I willingly give it my permanent and lifetime commitment." Of course, some people can say the above, but then not act it out in everyday life. To make this statement reflect reality a person must be *congruent* rather than *contradictory*, which means that his/her actions must support the words!

Does it matter what you are passionate about? No, as long as it is life-affirming, feeds real needs, and does no harm. This only means that serial killers and con men can be passionate about their activities, but destructiveness, by definition is not creative. While destroying is always easier than creating, it can never build internal happiness.

The appeal of being destructive is that it can be exciting, and to a person without consciousness and caring, destroying can bring a momentary feeling of passion and power. Historically, people have wanted to experience *feelings* of passion and power, even if only momentary, so destructiveness has had its advocates in every generation.

Being creative requires life-affirming passion and purposes, but other than this the possibilities are nearly infinite. What you choose to pursue with whole-hearted passion matters less than feeding your *need* to be passionate in your preferences. So whether you love people, plants, animals, art, photography, sports, fashion, culinary arts, or whatever else matters less than that you *love whole-heartedly* and are committed to your purposes and preferences.

In loving a specific aspect of life you create a focus point to channel your effort and energy, and discover your unique talent. One consequence of identifying *passionate preferences* is that it provides activities to *master* that build layer upon layer of lasting satisfaction and genuine meaning.

Mastery & Passionate Preferences

Creatively mastering the awareness and skills associated with passionate preferences provides one of life's most enduring of all satisfying experiences. A favorite belief of the mediocre and inadequate, however, is they can be *creative* without *working* for mastery. If you were to ask the four icons, they would all tell you that hard work is the backbone of mastery, and that both hard work and mastery are essential keys to timeless expressions of authentic creativity.

So, whether you choose to master loving people or art, a sport, music, or any other life-affirming pursuit, internal happiness requires that you work to master the skills and awareness necessary to experience and express your unique gifts and talents. This is all part of the fun.

Of course, my saying that mastery is needed for creativity and that both are required for internal happiness does not make it true—so look around you and note those people who have passionate preferences and work to master them versus those who do not. Also, observe yourself to see whether you have identified passionate preferences and acquired the awareness and skills necessary to pursue and develop them.

If you have grown into your passionate preferences, what do you see are the consequences? For instance, do you derive a greater sense of satisfaction and meaning from defining and mastering *passionate preferences,* or from having a "whatever" attitude where you *hang-out* and pass the time? Do you see any difference in the experience of caring about and working hard to master your passions as opposed to being focused solely on survival and entertainment?

The Internal Potential To ***Contribute***

Making a contribution does not even become an issue until someone develops an external or internal abundance. Normally people wait until their *golden years* when they have an external abundance, like more money than they can ever hope to spend, before they begin to think about contribution, and then it is usually in terms of giving money. Even more seldom, however, do people develop enough *internal* abundance to make a *contribution* based on their *understanding, caring, mastery, and creativity.*

When I was 43 and eight years into private practice as a clinical psychologist, and my father was 70 and comfortably retired, I asked him, "Dad, if you could get a million dollars, or create something that would benefit human beings for a thousand years, which would you prefer?" He replied, "I would want the million dollars." This response perplexed me, so I asked, "What would you do with the million dollars?" He replied, "Nothing, just have it."

Now I was feeling shocked, so I asked, just to be sure there was no miscommunication, "Okay, so you would not use the money to buy anything, and you would give up the opportunity to help human beings for a thousand years just to have this money in the bank?" And he replied, "Yes."

Some people would explain my father's choice by explaining that he was a product of the Great Depression, and to some extent that is accurate. The issue is deeper than that, however, because my Dad was financially comfortable, and really had no desire to have more material things or expensive experiences. Instead, the real issue was that my Dad did not have the internal abundance, or enduring happiness necessary to create the *desire* to *contribute t*o other people. This narcissistic and miserly attitude is all too normal, and far more prevalent than most people usually care to observe.

The reason is simple, many people never have enough to feel *externally* safe and completely full, but most people, regardless of how much wealth they acquire, do not fulfill their potential for understanding, caring and mastery well-enough to make a single *internal* contribution.

In other words, unless you are internally developed and truly happy yourself, it is unlikely that you will develop either the desire or competence required to *contribute* love and wisdom. For most normally trained people, all their energy is spent just getting through the day, feeling good, and being entertained; so they fail to have an internal abundance to offer anyone.

The problem for my father was that he did not fulfill his potentials—internal or external. He did well-enough to achieve some feeling of security—but not internal fulfillment. One consequence is that he was not happy with himself, or life, so caring about other people, whether his first-born son or the family of human beings, was not something that appeared as even a small blip on the radar screen of his undeveloped mind.

For anyone who wants to fulfill this critical internal potential the place to start is with the people closest to us; family and friends first, and then business associates and familiar strangers. Everyone needs whole-hearted energy and interest offered with genuine skill and innocence. When we contribute by feeding this need in other people, we expand our world in a most satisfying and productive manner. Being internally productive by creating satisfaction and meaning for ourselves and giving to other people enhances our happiness until the experience of internal fulfillment is consistent and constant.

Another way to contribute internally is to make it our responsibility to understand the complexity of our modern world and its problems. Mother Nature is declining in every respect. This means that Planet Earth has a finite number of life support systems essential to sustaining mammalian life, and right now, every system is under attack and declining. Human life is sustainable on Planet

Earth only because of a narrow range of temperature, atmosphere, resources, soil, and water. If these life support systems continue to diminish until they fail, or just fall below the narrow range required to sustain human life, Planet Earth will blithely go on her merry way, but human beings will become extinct.

If you care about what is happening to your only home, Planet Earth, or you would simply prefer to die a natural death rather than be an integral part of the next ***extinction event***, you can *contribute* to life by becoming informed until you truly understand the issues. The more people are aware of the complexity of the issues now facing our planet the greater chance we have to agree on the problems and work together toward solutions. On the other hand, the more we are passive and accept slogans, distortions, or simplistic solutions as slimy substitutes for real understanding, the more likely it is that we will never even agree on the facts, much less on how to respond.

Right now, human life is in jeopardy. Our environment and institutions—financial, political, medical, business, and educational—are all threatened, threatening, or challenged. Our normal process is to react with short-term and always inadequate simplistic solutions. Few people, individuals or institutions, are capable of thinking in terms of how to not only create a world where life is sustainable, but a world where internal happiness is the norm, not the exception.

Even if the world as we know it has a short future it is still everyone's responsibility, and in everyone's best interest to develop his/her mind and emotions and create internal happiness. Whether it is the end of the world, or the beginning of a new era—mastering happiness is the best response!

PART TWO:

Understanding & Nurturing Internal Needs

The Need for Primal Experience And Quintessential Moments

A conscious connection to the experience of being alive frightens most people. One reason for fear is that the facts of human life are brutal. To begin, we are all born with a death sentence. Next, there is no apparent purpose for human life, which means we must create one, or do without. Finally, just when we learn enough about living to do it well, *it's time to die*! Ironically, like in a Greek tragedy, everything we struggle for a lifetime to acquire or experience is lost when we drop anonymously into the abyss of eternal oblivion—not a pretty picture.

If we allow the brutal facts to touch us, even for a moment, then we can empathize with the universal human desire to use ideas, beliefs, or feelings to paint a prettier picture of life than observable facts will allow. Throughout history, people have created religions, mythologies, and spiritual beliefs to protect themselves from consciously acknowledging and emotionally experiencing the full force of life's brutal facts. The only problem is that in protecting ourselves from the brutal side of reality, we also make it impossible to experience the full impact of life's joy and wonder.

It is important to notice that joy and wonder are emotions that people only have a *potential* to experience. Unfortunately, these positive experiences are *optional*. By contrast, the negative or painful facts of life are compulsory and inescapable. As a result, we can ignore the negative and pretend that it does not exist, but no one escapes the experience of pain, loss, and death. Since no one escapes life's pain, it is time to understand that anyone who wants to grow, or build internal happiness, must also acknowledge the negative.

The task is to begin by observing everything life offers, and in spite of the dreary side, whole-heartedly engage each experience with the purpose of wanting to see and understand reality—*pleasant and painful*. Fulfilling this purpose requires a *conscious connection* to the entire gamut of human experience. ***A conscious connection to life begins with mastering primal experience.***

Defining Primal Experience

What makes *primal* different from *normal* experience? For one, creating primal experience requires that we engage our minds, emotions, and senses. This means that when listening to music, walking through a forest, in conversation, reading a book or watching a movie our senses are wide awake, our minds are innocently receptive taking in the moment and actively searching for what it may mean, and our emotions are authentically responding to all that is happening.

This conscious picture contrasts sharply with how we normally respond to experience. With normal training, we tend to emphasize one aspect of experience over another. For instance, we sometimes choose to emphasize ideas over both emotions and senses, and as a result, disconnect from life by intellectualizing experience. At other times, we exaggerate feelings and become sappy or sentimental. This choice provides an excuse to obsess over every superficial or trivial feeling. Finally, we sometimes exaggerate sensory experience and live primarily for sensual pleasure disconnected from both thought and caring.

In each instance one function dominates, so our awareness is fragmented and incomplete. Creating primal experience offers an option that is more complete and balanced. When our experience is primal we learn to integrate mental, emotional, and sensual functioning. This means we keep all three functions constantly busy connecting thoughts, facts, and feelings—each operating in harmony with the others.

Everyone has the option to develop his mind, emotions and senses equally, or to exaggerate one function over another and become intellectual, sentimental, or hedonistic. Normally, people choose exaggeration over development. This means a person can spend time in nature but so *intellectualize* the experience he is not touched, taught, or fulfilled. Or someone can be so *lost in sentiment* that nothing in nature can penetrate the self-absorption. Other people prefer to exaggerate sensual pleasure. The only problem in becoming a hedonist is that being in nature is sometimes uncomfortable, which for a hedonist can take the fun out of the experience.

When we develop our minds, emotions, and senses equally, so each function is trained to work competently and in harmony with the others, every new moment becomes a visceral experience that is unique and complete.

For instance, in making experience primal, we first train our minds to be a clearly focused, delightfully receptive, and finely tuned consciousness. At the same time, we also develop caring that is whole-hearted and a reliable source of renewable energy. Finally, we train our senses to be awake and aware and constantly providing a steady flow of accurate information about the objective world and everyday reality.

After retraining our minds, emotions and senses, being in nature becomes a *primal* experience that fills our consciousness with color, light, sound, and touch. Now, we innocently *respond* to the experience of natural life with feelings of wonder and joy. With every experience, our minds acknowledge that even moments of pure joy and innocent wonder include the inescapable sadness of knowing there is nothing we get to keep, or control.

An important *principle of life* is revealed when we spend time in nature: ***All truly significant experiences contain both joy and sadness.*** If we acknowledge that joy and sadness are inseparable, *and choose to experience life anyway*, then we are receptive to primal experience. We will also become competent to offer tenderness and comfort. Surprisingly, ***if we ever want to both experience and express tenderness, we must be aware that joy and sadness are inseparable.***

Defining Quintessential Moments

The ultimate primal experience is a quintessential moment. ***A quintessential moment occurs whenever an experience is internally and externally perfect.***

In part, *perfect* simply means *complete and timeless*. For instance, a perfect moment in nature might be a fall day when the colors are bright, the breeze is cool, the leaves are rustling in the trees, the birds are singing, the animals are scurrying about, and the intense beauty so fills our minds, emotions, and senses that we ache with fulfillment.

In addition to perfect circumstances, quintessential moments require our minds to be relaxed, but focused. Also, our emotions must respond with whole-hearted caring, and our senses must be alert and receptive. When both internal and external components are complete, we experience a truly timeless and totally fulfilling quintessential moment.

Everyone needs quintessential moments to create a concrete and visceral connection to life at its best, so in the end, when leaving life, we are comforted and fulfilled by having consciously experienced the heart of what being alive offers. We also need the *timeless* quality of quintessential moments. When an experience is perfect and complete, not only in terms of our own life's time, but for any time in history, then we experience true *timelessness*. ***Consciously creating quintessential moments is crucial to feeding our need for an "experiential" connection to eternity.***

Of course, creating quintessential moments requires an attitude of *innocent consciousness*. Innocence is needed so we focus on the experience, not the outcome. Consciousness is needed so our minds are concentrated and focused. Opportunities for creating quintessential moments occur daily in conversations with our mates, children, and friends. We can elevate ordinary moments by giving them our whole-hearted attention and creating a visceral connection to not only our own experiences, but also the experiences of other people.

It is important to notice that quintessential moments can be created by listening to music, reading a book, watching a movie, interacting with animals, decorating a home, walking in nature, or feeding any real need.

What Makes Primal & Quintessential Important?

There are many reasons to master primal experience and quintessential moments, but one critical reason is to experience a visceral connection to the mystery of being alive. Without the energy that comes from experiencing the pure joy and innocent wonder of quintessential moments, natural aging and the brutal facts of life eventually wear everyone down, break through even the best defenses of denial and avoidance, and make life more burdensome than fulfilling. You can observe this process here in America where many millions of people have everything external life offers, but little internal development and few quintessential moments.

One consequence of having every material thing but few quintessential moments is that people try to escape the reality of disappointment and boredom. In fact, we see people fleeing reality *en mass* as Americans lose themselves in food, alcohol, work, drugs, vapid entertainment, and frantically busy lifestyles that are pathetically empty of any conscious purpose, enduring satisfaction, or genuine meaning.

In frantically trying to escape reality people often lose awareness and caring, but ironically, retain anxiety and fear! We see a lack of awareness and caring as people choose activities and create conversations that have no conscious purpose, and provide neither satisfaction nor meaning.

If you master primal experience and quintessential moments, you will also develop *passionate preferences*. Now, you genuinely care how you spend time, and develop a burning desire to create meaningful activities. The days of wanting to squander the lion's share of your discretionary time engaged in trivial pastimes are over and gone, forever.

Understanding Primal & Quintessential

Understanding primal experience requires that we find easily available examples. For instance, anyone who has access to a library and observed pictures, or seen in person Michelangelo's pieta, statue of David, or the Sistine Chapel has firsthand knowledge that Michelangelo experienced life on a primal level. In viewing his work it is instantly obvious that he translated primal experience into timeless works of art that provide quintessential moments to anyone willing to *innocently receive* and *consciously respond* to his genuinely authentic and sublimely original creations.

Michelangelo turned paint and marble into an intensely personal and gloriously sensual experience conceived with intelligence and backed-up by power and passion. In studying his art, you can see primal experience beautifully expressed and vibrantly alive. The trick is to learn how to do the same yourself!

What we need to learn from Michelangelo is how to create our own primal experience of being alive. Of course, defining and integrating the attitudes of *curiosity, innocence, and responsibility* is a fine place to begin. If we study Michelangelo's life, we see he was a master of all three attitudes. Then, mastering the mental tools so *understanding* finds a permanent home in our minds and consciousness is another critical step. Next, we need to study ordinary life with the purpose of learning—just like Michelangelo did—how to be authentic and original.

In watching movies, look for moments that teach you about ordinary life in an extraordinary way. For instance, in the movie ***Out of Africa*** there is a scene between Robert Redford and Meryl Streep where they are in a tent making love for the first time. They have been slowly leading up to their sexual connection with layer upon layer of personal conversations and shared experiences with nature, stories, and music that in this critical moment releases a crescendo of passion that has been building over a long period of time.

In this intense scene, Robert is on top of Meryl and presumably inside of her when he looks into her eyes and says "*Don't move.*" She replies, "*But, I want to move.*" He says again, "*Don't move.*" Being unexpectedly still in a passionate moment, and then looking directly into one another's eyes, the experience becomes *agonizingly personal* and *intensely real.*

Normally, we expect sex to be *passionate and pleasurable,* not agonizingly personal and intensely real. What we fail to realize is that we need our sexual connections and our lives to be agonizingly personal and intensely real, and if they are, then both sex and our daily lives become not only passionate and pleasurable, but also deeply satisfying and meaningful to a degree that we previously could not have imagined. *Trust me; any couple who introduces agonizingly personal and intensely real connections into their sexual life will quickly find any other experience to be a cheap substitute, and sadly lacking*!

One consequence of experiencing this degree of intimacy is that ordinary moments are permanently etched into our minds and memories. In this example; the emotions, minds, and senses of this couple are engaged in a searing experience of shared hunger and personal passion that never loses its meaning. So, how often do you *consciously* experience such moments? Next, can you *purposefully* make these moments happen on a regular basis, or are you dependent upon luck and serendipity for them to happen accidentally, once or twice in a lifetime?

When you understand primal experience and quintessential moments you can spend every day in a world that is agonizingly personal and intensely real. Anyone who wants to become genuinely loving and wise must learn to live in this world. To verify my statement just observe any person, living or dead, who seems to embody love and wisdom. Then study their lives to see if they express love and wisdom over their lifetime. Finally, note whether or not they seemed to have a *primal connection* and *visceral response* to the mysterious experience of just being alive.

Over my lifetime, I have made primal connections to life a primary priority and conscious purpose. At a very young age it seemed clear to me that any other choice was a waste of precious time. My response has been to find various ways to live in an ordinary world filled with primal experience and quintessential moments.

Of course, moments like the one between Meryl and Robert require a consenting partner, and are not always available. On the other hand, we can read books, watch movies, see Michelangelo or listen to Beethoven, Mozart, and Hayden, or spend time in nature totally independent and all alone.

When I lived alone in the mountains of southwestern Utah for ten years, I had many an experience watching heavy snowfalls and dramatic thunderstorms, cross-country skiing, hiking, classical music, reading, writing, and watching movies and each experience provided intense delight in being alive in a context of sometimes agonizing loneliness.

One evening I was in the hot tub on my front deck with a view of a stream meandering through the valley below and a forested hill on the other side of the valley with pink cliffs in the distance. It was just past dusk and the stars had come out all bright and fresh and Orion was sparkling right overhead when a male deer walked past, perfectly relaxed, casually grazing here and there on aspen leaves and tufts of grass.

The moment was perfect and complete. The deer was relaxed with my presence because according to his perception a naked man in a hot tub might be a strange and unfamiliar creature, but certainly no threat! For me, just the experience of the hot water on my skin helped to ease the loneliness of having no one to touch or be touched by, and the deer was comfortingly like me, a wild creature all alone. My mind, emotions and senses were all present and engaged, so the moment is as fresh now as when it happened. What do you think; are primal experiences and quintessential moments worth the effort?

Developing Self-Worth In Children and Adults

Creating self-worth is required for emotional security and peace of mind. While everyone knows that self-worth is important, as far as I know, no one has clearly defined the specific steps necessary to create it. Instead, people assume they can create self-worth by getting approval, or by *believing* they have value. In normal life, we often assume that manipulating our beliefs and feelings is a critical key to acquiring internal value.

One problem with beliefs and feelings is they are *fantasy-based*, while real self-worth requires a *fact-based* internal and external *competence*. Since it is far easier to manipulate beliefs or feelings than become competent, we are often reluctant to acknowledge that developing genuine self-worth requires that we master both internal and external needs and potentials.

With normal training, we are often taught to believe that everyone has value. We reframe the whole issue if we acknowledge that it is possible to be worthless! While this is not true for children because they are truly helpless, it is true for legions of adults who feel or act helpless, when in fact they are not helpless, just poorly trained and internally inadequate.

The primary problem is that adults must earn their value, in part by mastering all real needs. It is important to notice that failure to master our needs—in spite of any belief or feeling to the contrary—does in *fact* sometimes make us *functionally* worthless to ourselves and other people.

Building Self-Worth in Children

Children develop self-worth differently than adults. This is because the facts of a child's reality are different from the facts that define an adult's world. As we have seen, one critical difference is that children are legitimately dependent on their parents for external survival needs, as well as every internal mental and emotional need.

The problem for children is that most parents never fully master their own needs, especially their need for self-worth. In spite of failing to acquire internal development, normal parents often assume they will be more effective than *their* parents at raising children, *believing* they can offer what they never received and still cannot provide for themselves.

One consequence of relying on assumptions and beliefs is that we often fail to see the contradictions they contain. As we have seen, many parents *believe* they can feed their child's need for self-worth even though their own is incomplete, but a moment of thought will reveal this is in *fact,* not possible. Unless a parent masters his own self-worth, he can never understand what his children need. Sadly, people rarely question a *belief* just because it contradicts observable experience.

Another assumption that most adults thoroughly accept is that *approval* creates self-worth. Relying on this belief, parents pursue approval themselves, and in turn, offer it to their children. Unfortunately, no amount of approval builds self-worth in anyone, child or adult. The reason is we *need* the information that acknowledgment and understanding provide, and while we *want* approval it is too judgmental and simplistic to provide even a shred of useful information.

In stark contrast, if a child receives *whole-hearted attention* in a context of *genuine interest* and expressed by intelligent questions, he will both learn and feel valued. If the parent also learns how to *confirm* and *clarify* the child's reality, the satisfaction for both parent and child will be complete. Giving our children attention and interest, along with confirming and clarifying their reality is a start toward feeding their *internal* need for acknowledgment and understanding.

Building self-worth requires that we apply the *formula for understanding* to acknowledging our children.

Formula for Understanding

1. **Identify a significant topic**
2. **Explore the topic in detail**
3. **Discover what is true**
4. **Use what we learn to *change***

Acknowledging children requires that we no longer try to *teach* them what is *right*, but instead, help them learn how to *observe, explore, and discover* what is *true and needed*. Parents normally teach by offering approval or advice, which is rarely useful. When subjected to approval and advice over time, children learn their parents have little of real value to offer.

By contrast, if parents master the *formula for understanding* they will offer acknowledgment that leads to understanding the child, and more about themselves and life. In the process, the parents will acquire insight until a particular child's motivations, purposes, needs, choices, and behaviors are clearly revealed. One happy consequence is that parents develop the competence to *consciously connect* with their own experiences, as well as the experiences of their children, family, and friends

In addition to the *internal* warmth of acknowledgment, children also need *external* warmth and comfort. For example, a home that is clean and comfortable will help feed a child's need for external warmth and comfort. If the parent's purpose is conscious, then the experience will also be internally warm and comforting. The reason is that creating a comfortable home with a *conscious purpose to nurture* feeds a child's need for both physical comfort and safety, and emotional warmth.

By contrast, parents can offer a clean and comfortable home, but if the purpose is for *image* rather than *nurturing*, then they create a cold environment where anxiety and tension dominate. Building a home for image creates a contradiction that confuses children. That is, to a child a clean and comfortable home seems like it *should* feel warm, so they are confused when the *experience* is actually tense and cold. This observation reveals that creating a clean and comfortable home with a *conscious purpose* to *understand and nurture* is critical to feeding a child's physical and emotional needs.

Next, we see that in addition to being nurtured by their physical surroundings, children also need to be consciously touched. As we will see, not all touching is created alike or feeds a child's needs, in the same way that not all touching feeds an adult's needs.

Self-Worth & Conscious Touch

Conscious touch is crucial to building self-worth in children, however, touching, hugging, or patting a child must be in response to understanding what the child *needs*, **not** what the parent *wants*. Sometimes, parents touch children motivated by a desire to satisfy their own hunger for closeness, self-worth, or emotional safety, but *explain* their behavior as being motivated by what the child's needs.

Children intuitively recognize this contradiction, and it is one reason they sometimes grow up desperate for touch—while at the same time—resist, avoid, or just become indifferent to the actual experience. Later in life, when these children become adults, they are often unskilled or awkward in touching their mates or children, which is one sad way this internal inadequacy is passed on from generation to generation.

A conscious touch acknowledges to a child they are desirable in an innocent and very personal way. Touching by our parents, when it is conscious and innocent, teaches us to be confident in our physical attractiveness and value. This is critical later on in life when we look for a mate. Children that are not consciously touched often suffer a lifetime of feeling undesirable, and may react by being obsessed with their appearance.

Both males and females will act out feeling undesirable by being hyper-sensitive to rejection, or trying too hard to please or be attractive to the opposite sex. The internal value a child develops when consciously touched by his/her parents provides a lasting and critical element of self-worth.

More about Acknowledgment & Understanding

A critical source for feeding a child's need for self-worth is the experience of receiving whole-hearted energy and attention from parents motivated by a *conscious desire to understand,* rather than the *normal desire to shape, mold, and control.* No other experience so convincingly proves to children they are valuable than when their parents take the time and commit the energy necessary to both acknowledge and understand them. Feeding a child's internal needs requires that we *give* the attention we have always wanted, but rarely received. This means that the normal half-hearted, trivial or trite questions are ***never*** *enough.*

Children quickly see that asking, "How was your day?" or "Do you like school?" reveal their parents as *trying* to appear interested when in fact their minds are distracted, or just absent. One consequence is that children respond with disinterested and one-word answers like, "Fine" and "Yes" or "No."

Parents need to replace the normal trite questions with intelligent questions motivated by genuine caring. Intelligent questions motivated by real caring require thought. For instance, questions like, "*What* happened today?" and "*What* did you do?" as well as, "*What* was your response?" require effort to ask, and more than one word to answer.

To make everyday conversation satisfying for children, parents must learn to *give* them a chance to talk, and then *confirm and clarify* their children's reality. ***When it is a parent's practice to preach, teach, and control it is impossible to confirm or clarify their child's experience.*** In a family with normally trained parents, children learn that a conversation with Mom or Dad requires they *give* attention, and *get* lectured.

For many children there is little reward for talking with their parents. This is one way that people unconsciously create a *generation gap*. That is, by the time most children become teen-agers one of the most unsatisfying experiences they can imagine is being a captive audience in a conversation with Mom or Dad.

It would simply never occur to normally trained adults that establishing a connected and bonded relationship with a child requires they become *competent* to make conversation a *personal* experience. ***Of course, the responsibility to make each conversation personal and satisfying applies to all intimate relationships—whether with a mate, child, or friend.***

Even if we do not have children, it is important to understand how to create self-worth in a child. The reason is we need to see how our parents expanded or diminished our self-worth, so we can identify what we need to provide for ourselves.

Self-Worth for Adults

In defining adult self-worth, most people discover they need to retrain their minds and emotions. All the principles necessary to build value in children also apply to adults. Only as an adult, we have to do everything for ourselves! This means that we need to master internal needs and potentials totally on our own. Each step toward mastering our needs and potentials develops another layer of internal competence; and with it our self-worth.

It is important to see that building self-worth as an adult requires that our perspective changes to fit our age and level of responsibility. Too often, we grow chronologically old while remaining stuck with a child's perspective, and this sad reality makes developing self-worth impossible. In the next chapter, we will define an adult perspective in detail, so we can see how to feed this critical need and master this developmental task.

Developing an Adult Perspective

In normal life, we define everything in terms of external experience, and an *adult perspective* is no exception. Usually, people assume that by acquiring an education, earning a living, finding a mate and establishing a family, they inevitably develop an adult perspective.

Even though no one specifically thinks about it, we often assume that *internal* development occurs *automatically*. The reality is that internal development has never been clearly defined, so it rarely happens. Instead, people become chronological adults with a child's perspective. Predictably, the consequences of acquiring adult responsibilities while remaining stuck with a child's perspective are devastating.

For instance, when choosing a career we often react to circumstances in the moment and then choose or fall into a job or profession that offers the most security, approval, or financial advantage. Rarely do we see that ***challenging our minds and emotions, experiencing risk and adventure, creating meaningful work, or making daily life stunningly satisfying and genuinely meaningful are the truly significant criteria for choosing a career.***

Similarly, we often enter romantic relationships assuming that a mate should satisfy our need for self-worth, fill up our internal emptiness, and make us feel safe and secure, which of course, is a child's perspective. With the absence of internal development, i.e. an adult perspective, it is not possible to give, grow, and share in a romantic relationship.

When people enter romantic relationships expecting to be nurtured and protected, conflict is certain. Unfortunately, the only way to resolve this conflict is if both parties develop the internal competence that defines an adult perspective.

Of course, one popular response to being disappointed with our mate is the ancient, "We should have children!" The hope *burns eternal* that a child will fill up the holes in our lives that a mate has failed to satisfy. What is remarkable is that if one child is not enough to fill up our emptiness, or instead, creates even more discontent because children have so many needs of their own, the skewed logic of a normal mind imagines, "Somehow, more will be better!"

Predictably, creating more children is never more satisfying, only more tragic. The problem is that when parents have a child's perspective then children are raising children, because no one is a mental and emotional adult. In the absence of internal development, parents inescapably pass on to their children a failure to develop self-worth, think for understanding, build bonded relationships, and master every real need and potential.

Facts & Feelings vs. Needs & Wants

Of course, developing an adult perspective is an incremental process. For instance, when we learn to rely on *facts* to define and feed *needs*—as opposed to impulsively follow our *feelings* to gratify *wants*—then we take a step toward developing an adult perspective. This step is critical because children confuse *facts, feelings, wants and needs*, and then impulsively follow their feelings. In a child, this is totally appropriate.

To become an internal adult, we need to *acknowledge* our *feelings* and *wants*, but *care about* observing the *facts* and feeding *needs*. Sadly, everyday life reveals that most adults blindly follow their feelings and desires and remain ignorant of both the facts and their needs. Of course, the consequences are always damaging.

We can see a present day example of this process in our need to protect planet Earth—because this is our nest and only home. We *need* to protect the air, water, soil, and every natural resource from damage or depletion, since everyone's life depends upon a sustainable supply of all four.

So far, each generation has followed their desires and depleted every resource without restraint. Consequently, life on planet Earth is now diminishing in **every** respect. The loss of Earth's vitality is a direct result of collectively *acting out* a child's perspective on a global scale.

People are proving through their choices and behavior they are *developmentally* incapable of caring about the earth's decline. The problem is that caring about facts and real needs requires an adult perspective, and as a group, human beings have clearly not developed beyond a child's perspective.

Another common example of chronological adults acting out a child's perspective occurs when people choose foods that gratify their *desire* for pleasure over their *need* for energy and health. Adults also reveal a child's perspective when they gratify their *desire* to fill up on images of impersonal sex or mindless violence—rather than feed their internal *need* for truth, beauty, meaningful work, conscious purposes and bonded relationships.

Restraint & Uncertainty

When chronological adults act out a child's perspective, making self-destructive choices is inevitable. Healing this contradiction requires enough *mental* development to *define* needs, and enough *emotional* development to *want* to feed them. These are critical elements in creating an adult perspective—that is, we must learn to ***want what we need***.

Growing enough to *want what we need* requires two traits not found in children. The first is *restraint,* and the second is the ability to tolerate *uncertainty*. The reason these two qualities are critical is that understanding our best interest builds slowly—layer upon layer, and insight upon insight. This process requires enough restraint to give energy and attention, over time and with little immediate external reward. Of course, the uncertainty comes in part from not knowing where either life or internal growth will lead.

With normal training, most adults fail to develop enough to tolerate *uncertainty* or apply *restraint,* so instead they *rush to gratification and judgment.* This is one way we often make choices with lifetime consequences based primarily on impulsive feelings. It is also how we come to repeat destructive patterns—that is, we never learn how to tolerate uncertainty or apply restraint well-enough to first define and then choose what is in our own best interest.

We can see that an adult perspective requires that we develop enough consciousness and caring to first define every real need, then to want what we need, and finally, to consciously choose to feed every real need.

Real Adults *Want* Internal Independence

As we have seen, adults with a child's perspective consistently choose to follow their desires, impulses, or feelings, and remain forever inadequate to feed even a single internal need. The pre-requisite for taking total responsibility for every real need is a *conscious desire* to be *internally independent.*

With a conscious desire to be *internally independent*, we commit to mastering mental and emotional development. ***It is important to remember that adult responsibility is total, which means that we are solely responsible for every need, want, pain, hunger, failure, and success—no exceptions.*** Adopting a no exceptions policy makes it possible to avoid confusion and accurately affix accountability.

In acting out a child's perspective, however, normal adults look for someone to blame for every disappointment, pain, hunger, or fear. You can see a child's perspective operating at every level of society; from the accountant or CEO with his hand in the money drawer, to the politician or theologian caught with his pants down. In each instance, we hear something different: Denial, "I did not have sex with that woman!" Excuse, "I didn't know!" Cosmic blame, "The devil made me do it!" Local blame, "I was betrayed by the office staff!" With an adult perspective, we finally and forever put to rest, "Who is to blame?" The answer to the blame question is *always*, "I am!"

Developing an adult perspective requires a conscious desire to be *internally independent,* which is very different from the normal desire to be *successfully dependent!* You can observe both males and females trying to get a mate, job, children or friends to feed their need for self-worth, fill up their internal emptiness, and make their lives at least feel meaningful.

Developing an adult perspective is a critical step in creating self-worth based on internal competence. The next step is mastering the internal need to feed our minds truth. This step is crucial because we all need the understanding and wisdom that only truth can provide, but we rarely learn how to feed our minds the ordinary everyday truth that answers the question, "Who am I?", reveals the brutal realities of being alive, and teaches us about the needs and potentials of other people.

The Need for Truth

One reason to master feeding our minds truth is that we need *energy* to innocently receive and consciously respond to everyday experience. As we age, our mental, emotional, and physical energy diminishes. This is a natural process, but it is exacerbated by failing to feed our internal needs. As a result, if we fail to feed our minds truth, then our energy is drained by the stresses of everyday life and not replaced, or renewed, so over time it is easy to feel more burdened with life than fulfilled.

On the other hand, *consciously* feeding our minds truth creates the internal inspiration and satisfaction we need to renew our energy. The reason is that we all experience a real need to grow in our understanding of ourselves, life, and other people. What makes feeding this need so inspiring is that our consciousness and caring grows with every new layer of insight, understanding, and degree of competence.

Learning how to use observations and reason to create precise definitions of internal needs is one way to feed our minds truth, and is similar to feeding children nutritious food so they grow-up healthy. Of course, if we feed children a diet of coke and candy rather than real food their bodies will not develop, and they will have no energy. Instead, they will become mentally deficient and physically sick.

A similar process applies to everyone's mind. That is, if we rely on beliefs and feelings to create foggy impressions, rather than observations and questions to create clarity, then we feed our minds distorted or inadequate information that only produces confusion, and drains our energy.

Sometimes, we become so accustomed to filling our minds with opinions and judgments that we doubt clarity is possible. One consequence of this normal tragedy is that many people now believe all truth is entirely *subjective*, which means they assume truth is defined by each person's subjective preferences, so it is meaningless to discuss.

Arguing whether or not truth exists is not new. Long ago at Christ's trial, Pilate asked Jesus to state his purpose, and Jesus said that his task was to present the "*truth*". Pilate responded by asking, "Whose truth?" Since Pilate's question revealed his intention was to argue rather than learn; Christ saw it was useless to explain, so he remained silent.

Defining truth is even more complicated now because of Einstein's theory of relativity, which states that an external fact is *sometimes* relative to the perspective of the observer. One result is the *International Society for Impotent Speculators* has what they think is a perfect justification for the eternally useless argument that *no* truth exists, because *all* reality is relative to the perspective of the observer.

Unique vs. Universal

It may be helpful in resolving the ancient debate about the existence of truth to note that some experiences in life are *uniquely* our own, and some represent *universal* realities. Unique experiences like our favorite food are truly *subjective;* or *relative* to each person because they are expressions of personal preference, or opinion. It is also true that some realities—like the four facts and internal needs—are *objective* and *universal.* This means that some realities are *relative* to each person's *subjective* preference or opinion, and some realities are defined by *objective* facts.

For instance, it is an objective fact that all human beings are born with a body, mind, emotions, and life span. It is also true that each person's response to these four facts is subjective. If you want to understand the complexity of human life, look for similarities and differences in how each person responds to these four facts. Next, observe whether there is a connection between a *conscious* versus a *normal* response to the four facts, and life affirming vs. destructive outcomes.

Your attitude needs to be *innocently curious,* because no one can learn while wanting to argue or feel superior. You also need a conscious purpose to learn from the experience of other people. As a child, I genuinely wanted to understand both life and other people. As a result, in elementary school, I read the biographies of many famous people so I could discover how they lived, the choices they made, and whenever possible determine the outcome of their lives in terms of the degree of satisfaction and meaning they created.

In reading the biographies, I learned that each famous person understood something about life, but not one had a consciously defined *internal purpose,* or directly asked and answered the question, "What, *if anything,* makes human life satisfying and meaningful?" This meant that each famous person's life was a combination of life-affirming and self-destructive choices that led to some satisfaction and meaning, at least a few internal contradictions and conflicts, and some degree of emptiness or confusion by life's end.

In my search for an answer to the meaning of life, I examined literature, history, religion, psychology and philosophy and found that human knowledge about living lies primarily in defining the "negative", or what is missing and unsatisfying, but no one I read clearly defined the "positives." This means that many authors describe life's tragedies or heroic moments, but not one I read clearly defined the precise steps necessary for internal development, including how to feed our minds truth, build bonded relationships, or create an *internally* satisfying and meaningful individual life.

The absence of a precisely defined process for creating a satisfying and meaningful life is one reason that famous people are just as vulnerable as you and me to genetics, timing, and circumstances. As a result, like any normal person, famous people create both fulfillment and disappointment. For those of us who are not famous, our lives follow a similar pattern. That is, we usually adopt a normal purpose to control security, approval, and pleasure; so even if successful in fulfilling these normal purposes we more often drain than renew our energy, and we are rarely inspired.

Energy and Inspiration

If you want to be inspired, and use the energy this experience provides, you need to feed your mind truth. Not the *ultimate, mystical, or spiritual truth* the Society of Impotent Speculators loves to argue about, but the *facts, responses, and consequences* that illuminate your experience of being alive. At first, pursuing truth seems like it should be desirable. ***In fact, how could a person not want to feed his mind truth for the noble purpose of understanding himself, life, and other people?***

Sadly, one reason people avoid pursuing truth is they want to protect their *beliefs* from being contradicted by accurate *observations*. Everyday reality can feel dangerous if it threatens beliefs that we rely on for approval or advantage. In addition, seeing reality accurately illuminates mistakes, so we see our every flaw and inadequacy in glaring detail! Few people *want* this information, even though we all *need* it.

Being Congruent vs. Contradictory

Everyone needs to observe facts and use reason to understand and master internal needs. Nothing is more satisfying or creates more energy than feeding our own internal needs, and then becoming competent to nurture our mates and children. In this process of development it is important to see that *understanding* requires we change any belief that *contradicts* observable facts. ***Protecting beliefs that contradict observable facts is normal, but extremely energy-draining and futile.***

One conspicuous contradiction created by normal training is that most people do not *want* to feed their minds truth. This normal but misguided preference creates a contradiction between the *fact* that we *need* truth for internal growth, and the *feeling* we do not *want* to master this need. The contradiction created by not wanting what we need is especially painful for family life. When we cannot feed our own needs, then trying to feed our family's internal needs creates irresolvable stress that drains rather than renews our energy.

If you want to build the energy necessary for real living, then feeding your mind truth so you become internally and externally *congruent* is necessary. Take a moment now, and ask, "Have I consciously created congruence or contradictions between my responsibility as a person, mate, or friend, and my level of internal competence?" If you create contradictions through a lack of competence to feed your own internal needs, or the needs of your family, friends, or profession, then it is time to feed your mind truth so you can resolve the contradictions and become internally congruent.

The more you become internally congruent by being competent to feed needs, the more energy you will have. On the other hand, failing to master internal or external needs creates chronic tension and discontent, and relentlessly drains everyone's energy. Feeding your mind truth and mastering internal needs cannot be reduced to a technique that leads to a spontaneous and magical transformation. Instead, feeding your mind truth requires a patient and persistent development that includes learning how to master the seven mental tools and the process of thinking for understanding.

The Need For Beauty

All experience is absorbed through our senses. In spite of this fact, in normal life we learn to *diminish* the importance of sensual information and to *exaggerate* the significance of beliefs and feelings. One consequence is that instead of connecting to reality by relying on accurate observations, we get mired in ideas, judgments, beliefs, and sentimental fantasies. When our minds are lost in a fog of fantasy we are unable to *innocently receive* or *honestly respond* to beauty, or any other experience that requires a conscious connection with the facts of reality.

Rather than consciously connect to sensual experiences, normal training so overemphasizes beliefs and feelings that a degree of mental and emotional *disconnection* from experience is certain. In responding to this disconnection, modern entertainment relies on loud noise, impersonal sex, and meaningless violence to capture the attention and stimulate the nearly dead nerve endings of a sensually disconnected population.

By contrast, with mental and emotional development, people learn to be *receptive* to their senses. It is important to notice that being receptive is a feminine characteristic that both males and females must develop before they can be touched, taught, and changed by the experience of beauty.

Life in a modern city discourages being receptive to our senses because the congestion, noise, and ugly surroundings are often overwhelming. What makes the surroundings ugly is the nearly complete absence of innocent life. Without open space filled with trees, water, plants and animals, all we routinely experience is concrete, smelly machines, noise, and of course, *too many people.*

Finding Beauty in Nature

In self-defense, we often turn our senses off and the background noise on, or even up, to distract away from daily experiences that are overwhelmingly drab and depressingly lifeless. This is just one reason that everyone needs to renew his/her energy by experiencing beauty in nature.

Walking up a mountain or through a forest we can take in natural colors, light, silence, and many forms of innocent life. The experience of nature encourages us to open our senses, so we can *absorb* the moment. Experiencing nature is one reliable way to feed our hunger for beauty, and in the process, provide a source of inspiration and energy necessary to renew our energy.

Can you bring to mind a moment spent in nature—perhaps a brisk fall day when you walked alone through a forest of pines, fir, and aspen? Did your eyes notice the bright and flawless azure of the sky above, the translucent yellow of the aspen leaves as the sun's bright light shines into and through each one, or the contrast provided by the dark green needles of pine and fir?

Now, walking on through the forest can you hear the silence that lies just underneath the sound of the wind as it makes the aspen leaves rustle, and the tall pines sway with a far-away roar, much like the sound of ocean waves crashing on a distant and deserted shore?

Can you also feel the gentle, cool, and refreshing touch of the breeze against your cheek? Do your feet respond to the soft comfort of the pine needles carelessly strewn in the path, or the alarming crunch of gathering piles of aspen leaves? Finally, are you sensitive to the subtle scents of drying leaves, warming pine needles, and the crisp cool humidity of a waning autumn and approaching winter?

If you contrast a walk in nature with the experience of a normal workday in the office that begins with driving on a crowded freeway or through congested and noisy streets, what comes to mind? In addition, if you compare a day spent with the innocent beauty of trees, animals, and all the color, light, texture and sound found in nature versus a day spent in the normal world of roads, buildings, cars and stoplights, which is more appealing? What makes it so?

Defining Beauty

One reason people consider nature beautiful is because we all have an internal need to experience innocent life. ***It is important to notice that we apply the word "beautiful" to experiences or objects that feed our needs, or gratify desires.*** This insight helps in understanding what often confuses people when they define beauty. That is, we often *explain* beauty in terms of the object rather than see that our needs and desires determine how we both define and experience beauty.

Remarkably, if we consciously take into account both the external facts and our internal needs, we can identify a few *universal* characteristics that define beauty. Of course, things like our favorite color, body type, or form of music, etc. are *subjective*, and are reflected in the old saying, "Beauty is found in the eye of the beholder."

On the other hand, the fact that all people experience similar internal needs makes it possible to define some universal qualities in beauty. For instance, we all need health, fitness, and a connection to reality, nature, and other people that is *conscious and personal.* As a result, if someone's body is fit and healthy, he/she has an active mind and truly cares about life, nature, and other people, anyone would say this person is *beautiful.* With this working definition, we are *responding* to *facts and needs*, rather than *beliefs and feelings*.

Now, compare a *conscious* definition of beauty with a more *normal* definition that requires believing in a cultural idea or form. For example, in following normal ideas or beliefs we are rarely content to define a beautiful body in terms of being physically fit and healthy. Instead, in trying to fit with cultural forms we sometimes use steroids or surgery to create bodies that would be more at home in a comic strip than real life.

If we learn to feed our need for beauty, we bring a sophisticated consciousness to the experience of nature, music, art, books, movies, and ordinary conversation. This is a huge part of the reward for *giving* our whole-hearted effort and energy.

The Need For Meaningful Work

Everyone accepts that survival requires work. However, people normally feel that work is a *necessary evil* to be eliminated as soon as possible. This is one reason we look with longing toward achieving *passive* income. It is also why nearly everyone agrees that investing our money—so we can spend our golden years playing all day, every day—is what *life's all about*! What is missing in the normal mind is a clear understanding of the role *work* plays in creating satisfaction and meaning, and perhaps surprisingly, renewing our energy.

It can be a shock to learn that becoming loving and wise requires work. The reason is we must *work* to focus our minds and emotions, then work even more to be *innocently receptive* and *honestly responsive* to each moment. If it is work to be aware of ordinary experience, then it requires a *heroic* level of work to master offering a personal conversation or conscious touch. As an ordinary man once said, ***"Life is truth, and requires work."*** We need both truth and work to use our experience of life to become loving and wise.

Most people prefer to avoid both truth and work, and one result of this avoidance is that few people can define and feed even a single internal need. Observe how people watch movies and you will see a contrast between *normal* and *conscious* attitudes toward *working* for the experience of truth.

Normally, people bring a *passive* attitude to the party of life, which is doubly true for watching movies. We usually assume that movies are for entertainment, and if we want to get our money's worth, we must be as passive as possible. On the other hand, if we observe that *life is truth and requires work,* then we bring an active *hard-working* mind to every experience, including watching a movie.

If you ask most people to respond to a movie, they may say, "it was *good*" or "it was *bad*" and not much more. If the person was deeply impressed, he may say, "It was **really** good, or bad." Not only will a normal mind express superficial approval or disapproval; he will have little memory of the experience, and little or no insight gained, reality confirmed, or lessons learned. Instead, it will seem as if the experience happened in a sensual, mental and emotional vacuum, and then disappeared down a black hole of oblivion—like most life experiences for normally trained minds.

The normal habit of bringing a *passive* attitude to everyday life drains rather than renews our energy. By contrast, if we bring an *active* mind that *loves to work* to everyday experience, then anything can happen. Now, we are open to the risk and adventure of passionately engaging life, where at any moment we may feel pain, tenderness, compassion or anger, or learn lessons that change us forever.

Everyone needs the risk and adventure that comes from working to bring every experience alive with attention, interest, and caring. When we watch a movie, we need to *actively* and *consciously* look for truth and beauty. Then, we need to watch beautiful movies more than once so our minds can fully absorb and integrate the experience. We also need to absorb and integrate movies that express significant truths. In learning to watch movies *consciously and purposefully*, we create the opportunity to practice the *processes* necessary to fully absorb and intelligently integrate every part of any and all life experience.

Whether listening to music, walking in the forest, engaged in conversation, watching a movie, reading a book, in the office or out on a job—all activities are a source for meaningful work. Only now, we accept that effort is necessary to feed our needs and renew our energy. We also see that normal life trains us to gratify our wants, while our needs remain invisible and unfed. This is what saps everyone's energy, that is, little-by-little the cumulative strains of normal life drain rather than renew our energy, and over time we feel empty, frustrated, or just sad.

The important lesson here is that the ultimate source for creating energy is feeding internal needs, and feeding needs is work. When we fully understand that feeding needs is required for renewing our energy, developing our minds, and creating internal happiness, then our attitudes toward work change.

When we understand its true importance, we *want* to work. We also *want* the responsibility to master every real need. Together, *wanting* responsibility and *wanting* to master internal needs creates emotional independence, and that, shockingly enough, provides more energy than it takes.

The Need For A Life-Affirming Legacy

Everyone's life is his legacy. This means that if we create *conscious purposes* backed-up by *congruent priorities,* then our legacy will be life affirming and meaningful. On the other hand, if we pursue *normal purposes,* then our legacy becomes a sad and self-absorbed emptiness that no one, including ourselves, can value.

Normally, people wait to the end of their lives before thinking about legacy, and then they think primarily in external terms. As a result, people sometimes try to get a school, library, or hospital named after them in order to *feel* they have a legacy. Sometimes, like Ebenezer Scrooge in The Christmas Carol, people decide late in life to become generous. The hope is that some last minute external generosity will compensate for a lifetime of being miserly with their time, energy, and attention.

The problem is we rarely think about legacy. Instead, we meander through life unconsciously reacting to circumstances without purpose or plan. One consequence is that life flies by while we focus primarily on *getting what we want,* and making ourselves as comfortable as possible. This often includes massive amounts of *entertainment,* which means we spend large quantities of time in perfect oblivion. In the end, all many people have to show for a life span is a few *good times*, a lot of self-absorption, and a sick feeling of futility.

Shakespeare felt this futility when he wrote that life " . . . is full of sound and fury, signifying nothing!" Most people eventually resign themselves to this cynical assessment, but paradoxically, also try to escape the pessimism with religious, philosophical, or spiritual *beliefs and feelings*. What people fail to ask is the simple question: "*What, if anything*, is necessary to make human life genuinely satisfying ***and*** permanently meaningful?"

This question is both honest and courageous, because it admits that it may not be possible to make human life either satisfying or meaningful. In addition, answering this question requires that we observe experience rather than rely on vague feelings or foggy beliefs. I first asked this question as a young child, and spent the last half-century observing facts, asking questions, making connections, and testing the results to uncover as much insight into the issue as possible.

One insight I gained is that becoming conscious, caring, and internally competent fulfills enough of a person's internal potential that some degree of genuine satisfaction and meaning is certain. This is true regardless of age, gender, culture, religion, social class, or political persuasion. The reason is simple: becoming conscious, caring, and internally competent is a response to life that feeds needs and fulfills potentials. In the process of mastering needs and potentials, we innocently receive and consciously respond to the experience of being alive.

One happy consequence of mastering needs and potentials is that we become *internally* competent, which in turn makes us mentally and emotionally independent, as well as useful. Being *competent, independent, and useful* are experiences that provide satisfaction and meaning, i.e., enduring value and lasting happiness.

Normally, we all pursue the American dream as defined by acquiring approval, success, security, and entertainment. Of course, if we fail to *get* what we *believe* is enough we consider ourselves unsuccessful. When we pursue normal purposes it does not matter whether we succeed or fail, either way, internal satisfaction and meaning will **not** be part of our lives, or legacy.

On the other hand, a life defined by feeding needs and fulfilling potentials lays the foundation for a legacy of contribution. With internal development, we build bonded relationships because of what we understand and are competent to provide. It is a fact that people value whoever feeds them. This means that if we master our own needs, and also nurture other people, then we create fulfillment for ourselves and build emotional bonds.

There is no greater satisfaction than becoming competent to create our own contentment, and at the same time, build bonded relationships with our children, friends, and mate. In normal life, almost everyone thinks he is eligible for the outstanding mate, parent, or friend of the year award, in spite of never consciously defining a single internal need, or becoming competent to nurture the people close to him.

Defining Legacy

As we have seen, legacy is what we leave behind, like the wake of a boat. While everyone can see the effects of a financial legacy, almost no one notices their *mental and emotional legacy*. No matter what your age, perhaps it is time to ask, "What am I leaving in my life's wake?" Answering this question requires that you assess to what degree you have mastered your own mental and emotional needs, and to what degree you have learned how to feed internal needs in other people.

With *internal* development, you create satisfaction, meaning, and fulfillment for yourself and leave in your mental and emotional wake satisfied mates, healthy children, and real friends. In the process of becoming internally developed you build truly bonded relationships with other people, so you are valued in life, and missed when you are gone.

Compare this *conscious legacy* with the normal experience. In normal life, many people, at least by middle age or after, are in the eyes of other people worth more dead than alive! By contrast, in our youth, we usually fail to accumulate enough money for anyone to care greatly if we are dead, or alive. How could it be otherwise, when we spend our lives perfectly self-absorbed and competing for advantage?

Spending a lifetime pursuing normal purposes leaves in our mental and emotional wake a disconnected and unconscious existence with no *internal purpose* or accomplishment. One consequence is that we often leave a corral full of frustrated or damaged mates, children, and friends—all who needed our attention, understanding, and real caring—but who received only divided attention, half-hearted energy, and the insult of empty sentiment rather than the meaningful nurturing of real caring.

Contrasting Legacies

I first began noticing mental and emotional legacy when as a child I compared my parents' attitudes, lives, and relationship with my Uncle Lon and Aunt May. What I saw was that my parents bragged about doing the *right thing*, and loved to criticize other people for being *wrong*. Of course, my parents never mastered the need to offer personal conversation or conscious touch. In addition, their attitude toward giving came from a feeling of obligation, not a desire to share or nurture.

Over a lifetime, my parents did fulfill a parsimonious idea of their external obligations to each other and their children. However, giving warmth, or sharing joy and pain were not part of the process. As a result, my parent's lives were internally empty. After spending over fifty years together and raising two children they were burned-out and ready to die, and no one mourned either person's passing.

Now, let us compare Mom and Dad with May and Lon. Lon made a living as a plumber in a small Missouri farm town. May and Lon met in their early thirties, courted for ten years, married, but had no children. Instead of obsessing about issues of *right, wrong, good and bad*, May and Lon talked about the experience of being alive. Lon was *respectfully skeptical* about religion, not cynical, which was courageous for the times and his circumstances. This meant that he would discuss life and religion with an attitude of wanting to understand, rather than adopt or criticize beliefs.

Lon actually talked to May—real conversations about significant issues rather than trivial topics. This was unusual for a man from a small Missouri farm town in the 1930's to 60's. May responded to

Lon by being a person in her own right, she asked questions and looked for answers in daily experience, rather than beliefs or feelings. Together, May and Lon engaged in conversation with an innocence and honesty that I had never before observed in adults.

Of course, I loved them for their innocence and honesty, as well as their curiosity, questions, and insights. My loving them was in some ways insignificant because they so completely loved each other. Not only did they offer personal conversation to each other, they also mastered conscious touch. I first saw them in their sixties, and Lon would still greet May with a big hug that included swinging her off her feet and kissing her with a primal passion that you would expect from a twenty-year-old.

It was clear to everyone that with conversation, touching and kissing, this couple was constantly growing in their ability to articulate and share the experience of being alive. Of course, whole-hearted loving always exacts a price, and the cost for May was that Lon died first.

He was fishing from the side of a small pond below the horse barn on my Uncle Floyd's farm. It was a warm summer afternoon with clear skies and just a slight breeze to make the day perfect. May discovered him, and it appeared to her that he had just lain back on the grassy bank and died.

For May, Lon's death was devastating. She was in the hospital for six months, and it was a year before she was herself again. I saw her about 18 months after Lon's death. She was genuinely interested in both my parents and me. May never mentioned her devastation, but would talk about Lon with longing, affection, and even humor when recalling things he had said, or moments they shared.

Hundreds of people from around the country sent their condolences to May. Lon, an unknown plumber in Macon, Missouri, had touched hundreds of lives with his kindly interest, irreverent humor, love of living, and passionate devotion to May. Two years later, May died.

Together, May and Lon left a legacy so endearing that thirty-five years after their deaths, I am writing about their lives and characters barely able to see the computer screen through my tears. May and

Lon's lives were their legacy. This is as true for you and me, as them. May and Lon were ordinary people who created internally fulfilled and meaningful lives. Their lives were their legacy, and their legacy was meaningful and endearing. If your life ended today, what would your legacy look like?

The poem depicts the **Life and Legacy of a Sequoia Tree**. First, look at the Sequoia on the front cover of this book and see if you can absorb the majesty and grandeur of a living thing that was alive and present, on the very spot where you now see it, when Christ was born! Next, read the poem, and note whether the description of the Sequoia tree offers something you can respond to emotionally, learn from, and perhaps apply to your own life and legacy.

**THE LIFE AND LEGACY
OF A SEQUOIA TREE**

You Stand Alone Without Complaint
You Develop Powerful Roots
And Reach For the Heavens
You Never Travel
Yet Always Grow and Change
You Endure for Centuries
Constantly Expanding in Strength and Dignity
While Your Graceful Presence
Nurtures and Enhances
Every Life under Your Majestic Limbs
And When You Die
Or Are Cut Down
One Small Piece of the Earth
Loses an Irreplaceable Presence
And Is Never the Same Again
PH, 2004

PART THREE:

Thinking For Understanding & The Seven Mental Tools

Thinking for Understanding
The Basic Process

Strange as it may seem, human beings have not developed a precise program to teach *thinking for understanding*. Sometimes, we teach problem solving—or how to get what we want. We also teach logic, formal reasoning, and something we call critical thinking, but we do not *consciously* teach how to explore ordinary experience until we *understand* our own needs and potentials. We do not even define understanding in contrast to explaining, justifying, believing, or theorizing. As a result, we often assume that acquiring an idea, belief, or feeling about something is synonymous with understanding it.

It is important to note that all understanding begins with *observing facts*. Most people accept that accurate observations are necessary to advance scientific knowledge. What is not so well accepted is that understanding ourselves also begins with accurate observations. For instance, to *understand* real self-worth, we must observe everyday life and discover each step necessary to first build a *conscious self*—and then create lasting value. Through accurate observations in conjunction with reason and thought, we can learn precisely what creates and destroys self-worth.

Thinking for understanding is a critical step on the ladder of internal development. Mastering this task requires that we adopt a *conscious purpose* to develop our minds and emotions in order to build a satisfying and meaningful life. This is strikingly different from adopting a *normal purpose*.

Throughout history, people have assumed that the primary purpose of human life is to acquire money, protect the status quo, and make life as pleasant as possible. A conscious purpose to understand our internal needs and potentials has not even been a file in most normally trained minds.

In science, however, *understanding* has been a conscious priority. The reason is that some people have truly wanted to learn about nature, and in the process of investigating the physical world they soon realized that beliefs, feelings, theories and superstitions were not helpful in actually understanding the complex world of nature.

Motivated by a *conscious purpose* to understand nature, scientists recognized they must develop a systematic process. They began by just collecting information through making accurate *observations*. Next, they used *reason* to connect causes to effects. Then, they formed a *hypothesis* about some process, or principle, and finally, tested their hypothesis for validity. The beauty of this (scientific) process is that no matter what the outcome, another layer of insight is added to our understanding.

Sadly, normal training does not teach us how to use the *scientific method* to first define and then master our internal needs and potentials. The problem is we are normally taught to adopt ideas, cling to beliefs, or follow feelings—but we do **not** learn to observe, ask questions, and then thoroughly explore and clearly define a single internal need or potential. Since feeding needs is required for lasting satisfaction, and fulfilling potentials is necessary for long-term meaning, we rarely become competent to create either satisfaction or meaning.

Mind, Emotions, & Senses

Our minds, emotions, and senses each have critical functions in learning how to think for understanding. This is one reason everyone needs mental, emotional, and sensual *development*, so each function is trained to operate competently, and in harmony with the other two. In normal life, developing internal competence is often impossible—in part because we learn to emphasize one function over another.

We have all seen *intellectually* oriented people rely on *ideas* for information about life. With an intellectual bias we fail to use our senses to observe facts, and our reason to explore what they mean. Instead, we create concepts that often contradict our actual experience. One consequence of being overly intellectual is that we are unable to define the sensual and emotional aspects of everyday life, or internal needs—like our need for self-worth, truth, beauty, meaningful work, personal conversation, conscious touch and emotional bonds.

While some people are intellectual, we see other people become so sentimental, or *feeling-oriented* they cannot *think* clearly enough to find their way from one side of town to the other. People sometimes use *sentiment* as a substitute for both *caring* and *thinking*, but sentiment can never replace the innocent energy and focused commitment of whole-hearted caring, or the clarity provided by true understanding. Consciousness and caring are required at every step of internal development, which is one reason we need to differentiate sentiment from caring, and then fulfill our internal potential to care whole-heartedly.

Finally, some people are acutely aware of their senses, but fail to master *thinking for understanding*. Hedonists and some artists provide examples. Sometimes, these people *feel* close to life but in *fact* fail to master thinking for understanding, so their connection to life, truth, and beauty is distorted and partial. ***Only an integrated mental, emotional, and sensual development will create a conscious, primal, and complete connection to everyday experience.***

Self-Assessment

To assess your degree of development, take a moment and try to define *self-worth*. For instance, describe in detail how to build a *conscious, caring, and competent self*. Next, try to define the process necessary to *build bonded relationships* in terms of feeding the internal needs for personal conversation and conscious touch, as well as for sharing reality, purposes, and quintessential moments. Finally, try to define the precise processes necessary to feed your internal need for truth, beauty, and meaningful work.

Examples of Exploring

For most people, it is impossible to define any internal need. The reason is that normal life does not teach us how to *think for understanding*. To develop *understanding* requires that we observe a topic, object, or person from many different angles. For instance, if we want to understand a physical object, like a pick-up truck, then we must observe it from the front, side, back, top, and underneath. Next, we need to take it apart and put it back together—if the doors open and close and it still runs—we *understand* the truck.

If we want to understand something more human, like the experience of taking our lover's hand, then we must acknowledge this may seem simple, but in fact it is a complex experience that requires specialized awareness and skill.

With normal training people assume that taking their lover's hand is a simple "grab and go" experience. By contrast, with training in internal development we see the need to establish an emotional connection through *personal conversation* as a pre-requisite to holding hands. This means we must develop enough *awareness and skill* to offer a personal conversation, and enough emotional restraint to wait for the other person to want the physical intimacy of holding hands.

When two people experience a *shared* awareness and desire, consciously enfolding each other's hand is satisfying. ***In contrast to an unconscious grab—conscious enfolding combines innocent desire with focused awareness to make the experience of holding hands intensely personal, sensuously intimate, and mutually satisfying.***

Mental Tools & Exploring

Exploring any issue, need, or problem is a complex task that requires mental tools to accomplish. The first mental tool is learning how to *concentrate* on one thing at a time, which is a fundamental skill necessary for thinking about any need, issue, or problem—internal or external.

Concentrating on just one topic is more difficult than it might seem. People often bounce from topic to topic and fail to explore any internal issue in depth. Sometimes, this is because they are so anxious their minds rarely slow down, or focus. Often, however, people just want to avoid becoming aware of their inadequacies and responsibilities.

Once you observe the *need* to concentrate, and practice keeping your mind focused, you can move on to the second mental tool—*making observations and asking questions.* In making observations you rely on your senses to observe facts, and your reason to ask questions. In asking questions, you learn to *explore* experiences and issues in precise detail.

Already, with two mental tools, you acquire three new layers of skill necessary to think for understanding. The three critical skills are *concentrating* on one subject, accurately *observing* facts, and *asking intelligent questions.* There are five more tools, and each one will expand your ability to explore. ***When you have mastered all seven tools, you will be able to engage any topic, issue, or situation and define the facts, explore the experience, and understand the needs.***

Identifying Significant Topics

In addition to mastering the mental tools, you must also learn how to identify *topics* worth understanding. One way to select a meaningful topic is by *observing* significant facts—like your own or someone else's age, marital status, or profession. If you concentrate on just one fact at a time, and then make observations and ask questions to identify in detail the *experiences, emotions, needs, and responsibilities* that accompany each fact, your insight into yourself, life, and other people will grow.

Your insight will expand even more if you *observe* how you *respond* to each fact. For example, you can ask, "How have I responded to the *fact* of being an adult person? Have I taken responsibility to develop my mind and emotions? Have I become competent to feed internal needs?" and, "Have I mastered my *internal* responsibilities as a mate, parent, and friend? If not, what do my priorities reveal has been important to me?"

As you ask and answer these questions you will discover what you care about, in part, by seeing how you have *responded* to the critical *facts* that define your life. You may discover that you have cared more about following impulses or gratifying superficial desires than becoming competent to think for understanding. You may even see that you have not consciously wanted to master internal needs and potentials.

On the other hand, with mental and emotional training, you will want to master your internal needs and potentials. Now ask, "What *response* to being a person, mate, friend, and parent would I prefer?" For instance, "Do I *want* to master thinking for understanding?" Next, "Do I *want* to master my internal needs?" and finally, "Do I *want* to be competent to nurture my mate, friends, and children?"

Your response to these questions will assess your *desire for development*. Without a conscious desire to provide the motivation, internal development will not happen.

Formula for Exploring

Understanding anything requires both mental tools and a *process*, or formula, so you have a structure to follow that allows you to explore any issue or event in enough detail that you can determine both what is true, and needed.

The Basic Formula

1. **Observe the facts of a significant topic.**
2. **Explore the topic using the seven mental tools.**
3. **Discover the critical meanings and needs.**
4. **Change to be in harmony with what you learn.**

To use this formula to understand a conflict with someone you love, start by *observing* the facts that describe the experience. Then, *explore* the facts until you *discover* what they mean and what is needed, and finally, make *changes* to feed the needs or resolve the conflict. Exploring conflict requires asking questions like: "What actually happened?" Next, "What did I want? Was I hurt, frustrated, or disappointed?" Then, "How did I *respond*?" In addition, "What did the other person want? Was he/she hurt, frustrated or disappointed? How did he/she respond?" Finally, "What were the *consequences* of each person's responses?" In addition to exploring negative experiences like conflict, this formula also works in exploring and understanding a *positive* experience—like intimacy. For instance, *observe e*xperiences that are in *fact* mentally and emotionally warm, personal, and mutually satisfying. Next, *ask questions* that *explore* each person's experience. Finally, use the information to *discover* in detail precisely what creates an experience of intimacy from each person's perspective. Then, make the *changes* necessary to feed this critical internal need.

As a teenager, I used this process in a very natural way to solve a problem that was at the time, near and dear to my heart. I began with the *observation* that at 15, I really wanted a girlfriend, but being naturally shy and quiet had no clue as to how to begin. After a little thought it was obvious I needed to explore the issue by observing boys who seemed to know how to attract and keep a girlfriend until I understood the courtship *process.*

At first, my observations revealed that *external appearance* and *internal competence* were critical to eliciting a positive response. This meant that physical attractiveness and cool clothes were essential. I also saw that the most successful boys were *internally competent* to offer a relaxed conversation, give attention, and make the girls laugh while not revealing a desire for anything in return. In addition, I could see it was in every boy's best interest to structure fun activities so his girlfriend consistently had "a good time!"

Based on *observing* and *exploring* the critical facts I *discovered* what I thought was needed and formulated a *hypothesis* defining what I must do to attract a girlfriend. Next, I consciously *tested my hypothesis* by making *changes*. Step-one was to lose the glasses. Hence, contact lenses. The next step was to get a surfboard. My purpose was to acquire a tan and muscles. In the process of mastering surfing, I spent one summer hanging-out on the beach with a group of kids where I began my *internal* education on mastering *the gentle art of superficial inter-gender conversation.*

After I could talk to girls and had done everything I could to be physically desirable, the next step was to buy a car and become mobile. This I did, and having accomplished my own make over, internally and externally, set out to find a girlfriend.

Of course, once I connected with Bonnie, I discovered that touching and kissing required another set of *skills and awareness* that once again, I was lacking. I discovered, for instance, that I had no clue as to what to do with my lips should they contact hers! Fortunately, after the third date when I turned to leave, in frustration, Bonnie grabbed me by the shoulder, spun me around, and kissed me!

I walked home, but my feet never touched the ground. This is one example of how *exploring for understanding,* along with a competent girlfriend, can create a satisfying outcome. In the next seven chapters, we will define the mental tools necessary to explore any topic to the point of understanding.

Learn How to Concentrate—One Issue at a Time

Predictably, the most basic mental tool in learning how to explore any significant topic is *concentration*. If your mind is unfocused and constantly skips from subject to subject, like a flat stone across still water, you can never observe any issue in enough detail to understand it.

Most people superficially slide from one idea, belief or judgment to another—rather than *concentrate* on a single experience and explore it to the *point of understanding*. This is one reason normal conversations often lack focus and become repetitive or silly. In an attempt to be socially correct most people follow the unwritten rule that demands they discuss only light or trivial subjects, *so everyone can have fun*!

In following this unwritten social rule normal conversations often bounce lightly from subject to subject, and rarely give any topic more than a sentence or two. People also follow another unwritten rule that says it is socially correct to avoid topics that acknowledge significant life experiences; like real needs, pain, death, joy, a purpose for living, or any *experience* someone truly cares about, or responds to with intense awareness and whole-hearted passion.

Surprisingly, the rules we follow to create conversation also provide the structure for our thoughts. The sad fact is that everyone's conversation mirrors his thoughts, in spite of the normal belief that we are more profound in thought than in conversation. Since what people say mirrors the content in their minds, we can observe that most minds lack focus, or concentration, and so—cannot *explore* any significant topic.

Methods for Concentrating

If you want to actually explore life, yourself, and other people until you understand all three, then you need to master concentration. This means you must practice focusing your full attention on one experience, need, or potential at a time until you identify all the critical details. Every routine event offers an opportunity to practice.

For example, in everyday conversation you can listen to what other people say, and then test yourself on how much you remember. It is important to observe that you will *remember* conversations that receive your whole-hearted attention, and easily *forget* them when you are distracted. As a result, if your memory is poor then it is probable that your attention is routinely divided, distracted, or simply absent.

Another method to help in mastering concentration is to *ask questions*. One reason to ask questions is to encourage other people to articulate their pain, pleasure, needs, wants, purposes and motivations, which provides insight into both people and life. Another reason is to give your mind practice in being active and engaged, i.e. fully *concentrated.*

Mastering the awareness and skill necessary to ask intelligent questions makes it possible to give the spotlight of attention, while you take the opportunity to learn.

For example, if someone says he had a satisfying vacation it would be appropriate to explore the details by asking, "What made the vacation satisfying?" Next, try going a little deeper and ask, "Was anything *not* satisfying?" Other avenues of inquiry include, "What *motivated* this person to choose this specific vacation? What were his/her *purposes*?" and, "What, if anything, did he/she *learn*?"

Do the details of someone's vacation seem insignificant? On one level they are, but on another just asking questions provides practice in concentrating your attention on someone else's experience. (A skill everyone needs) In addition, asking intelligent questions helps you learn how other people experience and respond to being alive, and illuminates the *similarities* and *differences* that you share.

You can practice concentration by giving whole-hearted energy and attention to every moment—washing dishes, cleaning the car, at work, playing sports, watching TV, or teasing your mate. You can use any task or activity to practice focusing your undivided attention with energy and interest.

Need for Concentration

Focusing undivided attention on every moment is contrary to normal training, which teaches people to judge their experience by labeling it *good, bad, pleasant,* or *painful.* One consequence of judging experience is we assume that only special moments deserve our undivided attention and whole-hearted interest.

One consequence of the *special moment assumption* is that an activity must provide a spectacular advantage or ego gratification to make it worth our wholehearted attention. This is why we hold sex, war, making money, and pursuing approval in such high esteem. That is, these activities are spectacular enough in pleasure, horror, or temporary advantage for us to feel they are worth our undivided attention.

The normal assumption that only a few activities merit our undivided attention is why we often obsess over sex, money, or approval; and at the same time, mentally reduce the ordinary activities of daily life to valueless burdens. Since ordinary activities consume the majority of our time and energy, once we devalue them with a divided attention and half-hearted interest our minds sleep through a large portion of daily life. Is it any wonder that as we age our days keep slipping away, faster and faster?

Focusing our undivided attention on each moment of every day slows the passage of time and expands our experience—because we are paying attention to each second!

If we want to slow the clock and expand our lives, we must consciously acknowledge that whatever the activity, it is still life; and being alive is fragile, passes quickly, and requires our full concentration.

Three Obstacles

To consciously receive and thoroughly absorb every experience we must master concentration. However, three obstacles present themselves when we try to concentrate. The first difficulty is that anytime we increase mental focus, we also intensify awareness of internal pain. Voluntarily increasing awareness of pain is not something most people are eager to allow.

The second obstacle to mastering concentration is that we start connecting internal pain with the needs that cause it, and it becomes glaringly obvious it is our *responsibility,* all alone, to feed those needs. Sadly, the only experience we avoid more insistently than an increase in pain is an increase in responsibility! Finally, the energy required to concentrate on reality leaves less time for narcissistic self-absorption, which is another change that our minds will often not tolerate.

Since concentrating on everyday experience leads to increasing awareness of both pain and responsibility, and reduces the time available to be self-absorbed, we often resist focusing our full attention on everyday life. However, learning how to concentrate, so we can *consciously receive and innocently respond* to each moment of every day, is necessary to see reality accurately and think for understanding.

Meditation

The most famous technique for mastering concentration is meditation. Usually associated with mystics, or a vaguely defined process called *enlightenment*, meditation is really a technique for keeping our attention on one topic. By itself, meditation will not create insight, or teach us how to think, but it is helpful in learning how to keep our minds focused.

Meditating on an idea or belief may actually retard the growth of our understanding. The reason is that ideas and beliefs are products of imagination, and no one can grow in understanding by focusing on fantasies. On the other hand, using meditation to concentrate on one topic, ask questions, and then use reason to make connections is truly effective in learning how to quiet our minds and expand our insight.

To master meditation, one method is to sit still and do one thing—be aware of your breath, repeat a mantra, focus your eyes on a material object, or your ears on a sound. Just being still and concentrating on one thing provides rest to your entire nervous system. In addition, meditation helps you discover that your mind is always active, with or without your direction.

Too often, we are so busy with multiple tasks, thoughts, and feelings that we rarely observe our own minds. This is how an entire lifetime can pass by and we remain strangers, to ourselves!

Initially, there are three reasons to meditate—one, to give our minds, bodies, and emotions a rest; two, to observe our minds and learn how they work; and three, to master focusing our undivided attention on one subject.

Concentration is the most fundamental pre-requisite for mastering all the other mental tools, as well as the larger process of thinking for understanding. Next, however, we will continue with the mental tools by defining the specific awareness and skills necessary to *make accurate observations and ask intelligent questions.*

Make Accurate Observations & Ask Intelligent Questions

Anyone who truly wants to understand life must learn how to *make accurate observat*ions and ask *intelligent questions.* For most people, the major obstacle to observing facts and asking questions is they do **not** *want* to understand! Instead, relying on normal purposes people want to follow their impulses, while also trying to avoid pain and responsibility. Just the ***idea*** of making accurate observations and asking intelligent questions with a conscious desire to understand is in opposition to the normal desire to feel free to follow every impulse.

With normal training, people learn to rely on beliefs or feelings to define reality, and then *sanctify* the resulting prejudices by calling them *right.* One famous example of this normal process happened to Galileo when the Catholic Pope decreed that planet Earth was located at the center of the universe. This seemed logical to the Pope because he *believed* that God chose human beings as His special life form.

The logic was that God would not allow His special life form to exist anywhere in the universe except the most important spot, the center. At the time, most people accepted this narcissistic nonsense because the Pope decreed that it was so, which in every believers' mind made it *right.*

Galileo ignored the Pope's prejudice and observed the motion of planets and stars in relation to the sun and respectfully submitted his discovery that the sun, not planet Earth, is the center of our solar system. Quite unimpressed, the Pope, relying on a belief that he was personally infallible, threatened to torture Galileo unless he recanted. Galileo wisely noted that what he said would not change the truth, but could save him from torture, so he recanted.

Observing vs. Believing

The situation that Galileo experienced happened a long time ago, but the conflict between *believing* versus *observing* rages on. For instance, only 95 years ago all wolves, bears, coyotes and birds of prey were considered *vermin*, and people *believed* that it was *right* to kill as many as possible. Now, we no longer consider it *right* to exterminate these species; in *fact,* it is against the law. What happened to change our attitudes so dramatically?

One significant event was that some people *observed* the *fact* that the experience of being alive is decidedly less joyful as we kill off all the interesting and beautiful birds and animals. In addition, we are learning that planet Earth is a *living* organism, comprised of subtle and often invisible interconnections. We are also *observing* the *fact* that Nature can tolerate damage or destruction to only a finite number of its interconnections before the entire organism—slowly, or perhaps more quickly than anyone could have imagined—disintegrates and dies.

What these observations reveal is that if people care about their own survival—then they must protect the survival of other species. The reason is that in a single living organism like planet Earth, the survival of any one part is dependent upon the survival of every other part. Of course, life on our planet does not experience a cataclysmic death just because one species becomes extinct. Instead, the earth declines slowly, like a person dying of cancer, as its *internal* vitality diminishes with every loss of *external* diversity.

Even these observations require a mind that can concentrate on one subject, and ask, "What are the facts?" These actions seem simple. Just *concentrate* on a single topic, gather information from your senses, and *observe the facts.*

In the two examples presented, we see that Galileo and a few Americans relied on their *observations*, acknowledged the facts, and acquired genuine insight. On the other hand, the Pope, and many normal Americans relied on *judgments* that distorted the facts to fit their ideas, advantage, or belief system.

In addition, both the Pope and normal Americans distorted reality in a way that allowed them to *feel* special, superior, or powerful. For instance, the Pope believed that because he was chosen by God, and therefore infallible, he was justified in imprisoning, torturing, or even killing any person who did not conform to his prejudices and beliefs.

Relying on a similar thought process, the American public *believed* they were *superior* to birds and animals, and assumed they had the *right* to exterminate whole species for their pleasure or temporary advantage. In both cases, observation reveals that any superiority human beings may possess does not exist in reality—just in their imagination!

History reveals that human beings have not observed reality accurately enough to define their own internal needs, much less the needs of other people or Nature, which shows a stunning lack of mental development—but no superiority.

We can observe a collective lack of internal development by seeing how Americans relate to food. As a group, it is obvious we eat more for pleasure or comfort than for energy and health. One result is that two-thirds of our population is overweight. Another consequence is that health care, the fastest growing segment of our economy, is devoted to treating illnesses that to a large degree (over seventy percent) are preventable.

We can see another example of our collective inability to feed needs by the fact that our cities—where most of us live—are ugly, overcrowded, noisy, and designed for automobiles, not people. This is one reason many people suffer from a chronic hunger for experiences with nature they cannot identify. One consequence is that discontent, depression, and addictions continue to escalate as people unconsciously react to invisible internal needs that are beyond a normal person's developmental ability to either define or feed.

The problem is we are so accustomed to relying on beliefs and judgments to designate what is *good, bad, right, and wrong,* we have lost the ability to use our senses and reason to identify what is both *true and needed.* People often ask me, "What is a fact?" then, "What is a response?" next, "How do I use my eyes and ears to see reality accurately?" In addition, "How do I observe?" and "How do I listen?"

Internal Independence

These questions reveal it is normal to be so *dependent* on someone else's authority or expertise that we fail to master observing for ourselves. To develop *internal independence,* we must use our senses to observe the facts, and our minds to ask questions until we acquire enough insight to create understanding.

Too often, making observations and asking questions conflicts with normal training. As we have seen, rather than wanting to understand, most people pursue simplistic answers. So like the Pope, people generally choose to justify their judgments and beliefs rather than accurately observe facts and ask questions with a *conscious purpose* of wanting to understand.

For example, it is normal to make crucial lifetime choices based on beliefs, ignore the choices other people have made, and never note the *consequences*! This means that we fail to ask, "What is required to make human life meaningful?" and "What, *if anything,* will make **my** life meaningful?"

If our minds are filled with conclusions, then we have no reason to ask questions. Instead, we make every critical choice by relying on beliefs or feelings. For instance, we usually *assume* that if we acquire a good job, nice house, sexy mate, beautiful children and long vacations, then our lives will be satisfying.

Now, stop for a moment, and observe people who have these things. For instance, do you see that even if someone gratifies every desire, he/she often fails to become relaxed, competent, wise, or fulfilled? In fact, achieving normal success often results in realizing you have every *external* thing, but still have an empty feeling in your stomach that says, "It's not enough!"

Seeing Self & Reality

This is where it becomes essential to make observations and ask questions with the sole purpose of wanting to see yourself and reality accurately. You can begin with, "What do I care about?" and then, "What is there to care about?" Answering the first question identifies the priorities that define your choices. This alone can be a shock and may encourage you to change. Answering the second question reveals what life offers, and may help in identifying what you need to care about.

In observing what you care about it is important to notice that *feelings* are not a reliable indicator. For example, you may feel you care about your mate, child, or friends, but if you observe how little *acknowledgment and understanding* you actually provide for them it may become obvious that your *feelings* represent empty sentiments not supported by the *facts* of your priorities and behavior.

Behavior, what you do everyday, accurately reveals caring. This means that you may *feel* you care about life, but have you mastered eating for energy and health and exercising for strength, endurance, and flexibility? If you have, then at least externally your belief is congruent with your behavior. If you have not mastered your physical needs, then this reveals your *caring* is based on sentimental *feelings* not backed up by the *facts* of your choices and behaviors.

What this teaches is that the best way to identify what you care about is to observe your behaviors to see where you spend time and energy. For most people—work, approval, and entertainment get the lion's share of their time and attention. Of course, acquiring possessions and a feeling of security are popular. Finally, we often devote time and energy to be with family or friends, even though our motivation is usually to **get** the people we *love* to feed our desire for attention and approval.

No matter what we learn from making observations and asking questions the act of doing both makes us vulnerable to discovering that the *concepts* in our minds conflict with observations of our *experience.* For instance, when tied to another person by blood or marriage, we often just assume that love must be present.

This means we assume parents love their children, and that being married for a long time *proves* the couple loves each other. If you believe in these assumptions it can be disillusioning to discover that real love requires awareness and skill. Even this insight acknowledges that offering real love requires enough skill to understand and nurture the people we love rather than offer superficial sentiments, or the often grandiose but utterly empty—*good intentions.*

Is it becoming evident that making observations will bring clarity to everyday experience, and requires courage? Courage is needed because we soon learn that nothing—not other people, life, or ourselves—exactly fit what we have been trained to assume, feel, or believe. One of the greatest obstacles to seeing reality accurately is the social pressure to adopt normal assumptions and beliefs. Of course, the power of social pressure comes from our intense desire to feel that we fit-in with our culture, peers, and parents.

There are costs to seeing reality accurately and thinking for understanding. One price is seeing that we are much less *special* than we ever wanted to believe. Another is that we no longer fit-in with all the normal assumptions, purposes, judgments and beliefs as totally or completely as we once did.

Intelligent Questions

In addition to *making accurate observations,* we also need to master *asking intelligent questions.* ***Surprisingly, normal education does not train us to ask questions, listen to the answers, ask more questions, and then change based on what we learn.*** Instead, with normal training we collect answers. If we do slip-up and ask a question it is often manipulative, as seen in the conclusions or criticisms that we sometimes hide behind a question mark.

One example of a manipulative question occurs when people ask their mates, "Why do you hurt me?" The *assumption* here is that our mate is responsible for our pain, and our *criticism* demands an explanation. Anyone who has experience with *why* questions can observe they often provoke defensive explanations or needless conflict.

Nonetheless, in spite of knowing the likely outcome, we still ask questions that begin with "why?" One consequence is the other person will first justify him/herself, and then counterattack. This oft-repeated process is one reason people become masters at justifying themselves, while at the same time never miss a chance to pin the blame on someone else.

If you can see that justifying and blaming create conflict rather than understanding, then it will be obvious that unless you want to argue, or make someone defensive, it is time to eliminate most "why" questions. Another reason to avoid "why" questions is because they contain the assumption you already know *what* is true. So, if you want to create understanding rather than justify, judge, or blame—then ask what, when, where, and how—**not** why!

One Question is Never Enough

One indication you genuinely want to grow is that your questions lead to answers that teach and change you, and then, you ask more questions. Normally, people stop asking questions once they acquire what they believe is *the answer.* This is an automatic reaction, and the predictable consequence is that we create primitive and simplistic views of life, and in the process acquire little or no understanding.

By contrast, every time we ask an honest question, we know the answer can illuminate only a small piece of reality, and we understand that more questions are required. Over time, the *process* of asking questions insures that our understanding continues to grow in both subtlety and sophistication.

Define Words In Terms of Experience

Words are like little paintbrushes in our minds that we use to draw pictures of reality. Like any artist, our minds need a model. If we want to draw reality as it is, then facts must be our model and we must choose words that accurately describe real experience. In stark contrast, with normal training we rely on concepts, beliefs, or feelings for our model—and we select words that create vague or distorted pictures of life.

The *primary purpose* for language is to transform experience, thoughts, and feelings into symbols so we can communicate with and understand each other. Fulfilling this purpose requires that we choose words that describe in accurate detail our significant internal and external experiences.

To experiment with the power of words, first *observe* a real experience, in detail. Then, *explore* the experience by asking intelligent questions. Next, think about what you have *observed* and *explored* and select words that accurately describe both. You will *discover* that language is entirely adequate to both describe and share complex experiences.

You will also see that effective communication requires concentration, accurate observations, intelligent questions—and *consciously* selecting words that paint complete pictures. Each step in this process is required to connect with and understand everyday experience.

Conscious Connections

Everyone needs a *conscious* connection to his own experience in order to build a *personal* connection with other people. If we listen to normal conversation it is soon apparent that people are often inadequate to describe their own experiences, and as a result are unable to offer a personal connection to anyone else. Creating *conscious* connections to life and *personal* connections to other people requires that we learn how to use words like fine paintbrushes to draw accurate and detailed pictures.

The process of using words to paint accurate pictures of reality that connect us to life and other people provides a life-affirming contrast to the normal process of using words to create vague or distorted pictures that separate us from life and other people.

Replacing the *normal* process with *conscious* connections can be difficult, but is not impossible, especially when the reward is opening a mental door to clarity and understanding that heretofore had been unconsciously nailed shut.

Defining Love

To bring a crowbar to that closed door in our minds and pry it open for the first ray of light requires that we take a word that is used often, but rarely understood, and then define it in terms of experience. The word *love* is a powerful example because all people have an internal need to give and receive love, and while everybody uses this word, few people even try to define it in terms of experience.

Instead, people admit they do not know what the word *love* means, but go on to use it anyway, *as if* their ignorance of its meaning is an insignificant detail!

For example, every child needs both acknowledgment and understanding to feed his internal need for self-worth. When this internal need is not satisfied, children experience painful feelings of insecurity and anxiety, sometimes for life.

While acknowledgment and understanding are critical to developing a child's self-worth, the sad fact is most parents do not consciously connect feeding this need with the word *love*! The inability to feed their children's internal needs and seeing them suffer is one reason many adults are frustrated, or stressed out by the responsibilities of being a parent. One sad consequence is that each generation passes on to the next an inability to even define love, much less offer the experience.

To break this ancient chain of ignorance and inadequacy, we must observe that children are loved to the degree their parents are competent to feed their needs. Most parents understand physical needs, however, in going up the developmental ladder to include mental and emotional needs, we start losing people—since very few parents can either define or feed their children's internal needs.

Perhaps you are thinking, "This sounds difficult!" If so, your suspicion is accurate. Becoming competent to offer the experience of real love by mastering the ability to define and feed internal needs requires time, energy, and effort. Sadly, becoming competent to offer real love requires attitudes and skills that with normal training people rarely, if ever develop.

It is important to notice that unless parents master their own internal needs, they cannot feed their children's needs. It is simply not possible to give a child what we are unable to provide for ourselves, even though we *intend* otherwise. If you observe this sad but commonly experienced *principle of life*, you will understand the meaning behind the trite old saying, "A person can never love another without first caring about him/herself."

Is it obvious that if we want to use the word love accurately, then we must define its meaning—not by looking it up in the dictionary—but in terms of experience? For instance, recall a moment when you saw someone innocently offer acknowledgment. Did you notice that asking questions with whole-hearted interest but no judgment was required to offer a mutually satisfying experience? Next, what were the consequences? Did the person receiving acknowledgement look relaxed, or appear to be satisfied?

After you observe that offering real love requires *giving* energy and interest, mentally review past experiences to discover whether you have mastered feeding this need in yourself. In addition, notice to what degree you are able to give energy and interest and not expect anything in return, ever! Eventually you will learn what love is, and is **not,** in terms of actual experience.

Normally, people use the word love without even attempting to define the experience. Consequently, people overuse the word, sometimes so they can exploit it for promoting an image. For instance, we often sell the *idea* we care by simply saying we *love* someone, and at the same time, hide the *fact* that we are utterly self-absorbed and perpetually manipulating for approval or advantage.

Once you master defining words in terms of experience, you no longer use words to promote sentiment, to hide the truth, or manipulate for advantage. Instead, you use words to reveal yourself and life as is, without exaggerating or diminishing a single point. One result is you become competent to observe yourself, life, and other people accurately and honestly.

Romantic Love

If we continue to define love in terms of experience, we see that after childhood our next encounter with love arrives when we fall into the timeless ritual of courtship and mating. Here, normal advice can be especially vague, sometimes silly, and always empty. For example, if you ask for help in how to choose a mate, you may hear anything from, "Follow your heart." to "Never mind, when you fall in love you will just know it." and of course, "You will know you are in love by how you *feel!*"

People often call these vague prescriptions *romantic*, and we see them repeated in books and magazines, on television, by our peers, and in school. Probably the most damaging idea is that love is something we *fall into.* Since love is something we fall into, it is easy to fall *out* of love when it no longer feels good.

Part of what makes romantic love difficult to define is that people often want a mate to satisfy emotional needs that were never satisfied in childhood. Relying on this motivation, we typically consider ourselves "in love" when someone is sexually attractive and seems to gratify our desire to feel safe and valued.

Disillusionment seeps in when we discover that no one has either the power or inclination to feed our desire to feel safe and valuable. Even with this information, we often resist the responsibility to become internally independent. As a result, most normally trained adults are to some degree, forever stuck with the internal neediness of a child.

One consequence is that people routinely expect their mates to satisfy needs that only their parents could have satisfied, and then, only when they were children.

If you want to grow up, not just get chronologically old, you must see that responsibility for feeding every internal need is yours, all alone. One consequence of acknowledging this glaring responsibility is that you define *love* in terms of what you need to ***give***, not ***get***. For example, in an adult romantic relationship each person is responsible for offering a definition of his/her purpose for living. In addition, real adults master their own internal needs, including being able to offer and receive a genuine emotional bond.

If someone masters his internal needs and potentials, he will become competent to create a satisfying and meaningful life, and will eventually become internally developed enough to grow, give, and share in a relationship with another person.

Growing, giving, and sharing are adult responsibilities that require internal development. Normally, people expect a mate to feed their internal needs, and often spend their entire lives as emotional children—pretending to be adults. With normal training, we often assume that our *feelings of entitlement* are sacred *rights,* and beyond question.

Tragically, contrary to what Valentine's Day cards and wedding invitations inevitably say, two halves never make one whole person. Only when two people are internally developed, so each person is competent to define a conscious purpose and feed internal needs—

as well as create an abundance of energy for growing, giving, and sharing—will the birth of real love finally become possible.

Are you beginning to see that real love is a rare experience? Can you also see that the absence of love—first as children and then as adults—causes much of the chronic neediness, emotional insecurity, and confusion that seems to permeate every level of society?

Defining Every Word

At some point it is natural to feel a desire to experience all the beauty, ugliness, joy and suffering that life offers. When this happens, we need to choose words that accurately describe each experience. The reality defined by the words *beauty, ugliness, joy,* and *suffering* may evoke strong feelings, blind assumptions, long explanations, or a blank stare. If we fail to connect words with experience, our thoughts may be filled with sound and tone, but will contain little meaning.

Is it apparent that once you begin the process of defining words in terms of experience, you need to continue until you define every significant word? This mental tool is extremely powerful in creating and intensifying a *conscious* connection to ourselves, life, and other people.

Next, to further expand our competence to explore, we will learn how to replace the normal *vague generalizations* with *detailed descriptions.* An accurate and *detailed* picture of reality is necessary to define precisely what is true, in part, so we can understand internal needs and potentials well enough to create enduring satisfaction and genuine meaning.

Details Versus Generalizations

Listen to any conversation, and you will soon hear that people prefer vague generalizations to precise details. There are three reasons for this preference. One, the more precise our picture of reality, the more painful life seems to become. Two, detailed observations of everyday experience reveal that we are alone and responsible, and life is a mystery. Three, when we define reality in detail, we soon discover that the facts often contradict our ideas and beliefs, which means that a normal model for reality is at least sometimes, pure fantasy.

Discovering that facts often contradict our favorite ideas or beliefs is one consequence of replacing *vague generalizations* with *detailed definitions*. It is also one reason that self-help authorities and new-age enthusiasts often feel a bit apprehensive about this mental tool. Of course, as long as no one creates a *detailed definition* for any real internal need or potential, then one self-help guru's ideas are as good as any other, so there is always room for selling more nonsense!

As a result, in the new-age world of *spirits, angels and feelings,* we never measure internal growth in terms of performance. This suits most gurus, self-help professionals, and the consuming public alike. The reason is that everyone gets to swim along in a river of vague feelings and gross generalizations with no risk of being accountable. To confirm this insight, observe your experience, and ask, "Have I observed many people who really *want* to ask questions that define reality in detail, or show they want to master consciousness, caring, and internal needs?"

Take a moment now, and try to define internal needs. You may discover that you have never thought about needs, and as a result, can produce only vague generalizations. You may even hear a tone of defensiveness or tension in your mind. Responding with a little defensive tension when caught being ignorant is a consequence of feeling that you *should* know, or *should* have the answer, and so being *ignorant* can feel the same as being *inferior.*

The critical fact is that being ignorant of internal needs is a natural consequence of normal training, which means that it is time to *breathe, relax, and learn.* Normally, if you believe you already know something, or just think you *should* know, then your mind shuts down with all the finality of a steel door being permanently welded shut.

The lesson here is that to learn anything, you must concentrate on defining daily experience with a mind that is relaxed, focused, and aware of being ignorant. With a relaxed attitude and focused awareness, but no predetermined ideas, feelings, or beliefs, your mind is prepared to accurately observe and precisely define every significant experience.

By contrast, we normally protect our ideas and beliefs—so vague generalizations are perfect for allowing us to *feel* we understand things that are in *fact* totally beyond our comprehension! In addition, vague generalizations are perfect for protecting our judgments from the bright light of accurate observations. Finally, vague generalizations are useful in avoiding the responsibility to feed internal needs—for example, when someone close to us is upset over our failure to acknowledge and understand them.

Asking Questions

Have you noticed it is rare for anyone to ask, "Do I give the people close to me all the time, energy, and attention they need?" Even more rarely do we hear someone listen to the answer, clearly define what the other person needs, and then feed his/her need. Instead, most people avoid asking for feedback. In fact, would you ask someone close to you, "Do I show you that you are loved, liked, and cared about?" If so, "What attitudes or actions do I offer that make you feel loved?" and "What, if anything, seems to be missing?"

You will notice that the first question allows a simple "Yes" or "No" answer, which was followed by a second and third question that require more *detail*. The reason for the follow-up questions is that people often hide behind vague generalizations. The gentle way around this defense is to ask for the details that illuminate the generality.

For example, if you share a painful experience with someone who believes he/she is sensitive, you may hear, "Oh, that sounds painful, but I know exactly what you mean!" A gentle, "What is it that you understand?" quickly reveals whether this person has a detailed awareness, or not!

You can compare asking focused questions that create precise and detailed pictures to the normal process that leaves people mired in murky generalizations. For instance, if you ask yourself, or other people, "Precisely, how does one make a long-term relationship with another person enduringly satisfying?" What do you learn? Do either you or other people offer detailed instructions that define precisely how to create satisfying relationships? In addition, do you see anyone identify the *specific* skills and attitudes that define his/her responsibilities? Or, do you see that people depend on vague *generalizations* to support superficial beliefs and sentiments about how to create a satisfying relationship with their mates, children, or friends?

Defining Friendship

My experience is that few people genuinely understand a single *detail* of their *internal* responsibility in making any relationship satisfying. For example, if you ask the question, "Precisely, what is required to be a friend?" can you answer with specifics? Then, continuing on to the next question, "Can you define the difference between *being* a friend, and *having* a friend?" How would you reply? Finally, how would you respond to the question, "Is it important for couples to offer each other friendship?" followed by, "If so, what makes friendship important to romantic partners?"

With normal training we often define a friend as someone we can rely on for a ride to the airport, or to pick up our car at the mechanic's garage. In addition, we go to parties with friends, share recreational activities, or like to believe we can *talk about anything.* Lastly, we often feel that we can borrow money from a friend, or ask for help in moving.

It is natural to define friendship in *external* terms, and by listing our expectations of what a friend should do for us. Of course, most people would say they want to give their friends everything they expect to receive. However, when first asked, few people define their *internal* responsibilities in being a friend. This example illustrates that a conscious purpose to *give and share* is quite different from the normal purpose to *get* approval, services, or advantage.

If you want to be a real friend, observe your everyday interactions, in detail. It will soon become apparent that while everyone needs and wants friendship, almost no one can define it, or claim to be internally competent to offer the experience. Another discovery is seeing that *being* a friend is more critical to long-term satisfaction than *having* a friend. One consequence is that it is in our best interest to define friendship in terms of what we are committed to *give,* not what we expect to *get.*

Friends Commit to Giving

Once you see that being a friend requires giving, it is essential to ask, "What . . . when . . . where . . . and how do I give?" Most people know how to respond to external wants and needs. On the other hand, it is seldom that anyone can both define and feed the internal needs that all people are hungry for a friend to understand and nurture.

Stop for a moment, and ask, "Do I understand mental and emotional needs well enough to be a real friend?" ***If you are unsure but want to be a friend, then listen to ordinary conversations***

until you see that undivided attention and whole-hearted interest offered in a context of genuine warmth and acceptance is necessary for friends to feed each other's universal internal need for acknowledgement.

After you see that undivided attention and whole-hearted interest are required, you can practice giving both to your friends. To be effective, you must understand, in *detail,* the *skills* necessary to provide a satisfying experience. For instance, giving undivided attention begins with concentrating on another person by keeping your mind both *intensely focused* and *innocently relaxed and receptive.* Next, you must combine undivided attention with whole-hearted interest. Surprisingly, this requires that you first learn how to give yourself attention and interest. Once you satisfy your own need, you must identify *selfish* reasons to feed this need in other people.

Selfish Giving

Developing a desire to **give** energy and attention begins with caring about your own life. You cannot care about someone else's life if you are indifferent to your own! Next, observing that life is a fragile experience where only death is certain helps in creating a *selfish* reason to give acknowledgment, in part because you see that in giving energy and attention you feed your need for *personal connections.*

There are other equally honorable selfish reasons to feed needs in other people. One life-affirming and selfish reason to give energy and attention is to grow in understanding. In addition, by giving experiences we have always wanted to receive, we feed our own need to be internally competent and useful, which further enhances our self-worth.

Consciously providing undivided attention and whole-hearted interest is important, but to be complete it must be in a context of warmth and acceptance. This means that if you want to express warmth and acceptance, you must learn to keep your body soft and relaxed. Breathing deeply and evenly, so that your stomach muscles are relaxed and your voice is soft and natural, is a good place to start.

These external physical qualities communicate to other people that you are relaxed and receptive, and genuinely want to hear what they are saying. Of course, in addition to being physically relaxed, you must also be internally genuine by whole-heartedly *wanting* to understand and nurture other people.

While it is critically important to develop the attitudes and skills necessary to understand and nurture, you do not need to be perfect. Instead, you must only develop your competence to understand and nurture to a degree that is *skilled enough*. If you anxiously pursue perfection, you lose innocence and spontaneity, and may create more tension than satisfaction.

As you explore the requirements for being a friend, does it seem that friendship demands more effort than you would have imagined? One consequence of replacing vague generalizations with precise details is that your appreciation for the complexity of ordinary life will grow. Normally, people cling to the familiarity of their mental *status quo*, which they create and maintain through adopting *simple answers for every complex problem or need*.

For example, in answer to the question, "Is it important for mates to be competent to offer friendship?" most people would say, "Of course, mates need to be friends!" Yet, how many people do you know who can define the complex internal needs and responsibilities of friendship in enough detail to master being a real friend?

Now, to make the definition of friendship even more complete, we must add—***being a real friend requires that we want to give energy and attention—even while experiencing emotional pain or mental confusion ourselves*!** This means that being a real friend requires *wanting* the responsibility to provide energy with little or no concern for our own pain, needs, or desires. How often do you see people willing and able to offer this definition of friendship?

Everyone needs real friendship, especially in the long-term relationship of being a mate. Here, maintaining an active interest in your mate, even when in pain yourself, reveals that your caring is genuine. In addition, consciously offering energy and attention, over time, creates trust and lays a solid foundation for building a bonded relationship.

Similarities & Differences

The first four mental tools are like the hammers, screwdrivers, handsaw, and pliers that fill a carpenter's tool chest. This means they are simple, but indispensable for building the skills necessary to master the process of exploring. The next three tools, beginning with similarities and differences, are like a carpenter's power tools, more complex, and necessary to build the layers of insight that create understanding.

Observing similarities *and* differences reveals multiple layers of motivations, needs, and purposes in everyday life. Of course, using this mental tool for the *conscious purpose* of understanding and nurturing is a world away from using similarities and differences for the *normal purpose* of justifying judgments, gaining advantage, or feeling superior.

In justifying prejudice, for example, people exaggerate real or imagined *differences* with the person or group they want to judge or exploit. This is how white Americans used differences between themselves and African-Americans to not only exploit them, but to *feel* superior. Then, to *sanctify* their prejudice and justify cruelty, they added the *belief* that God approved their judgments and exploitation.

People rely on the same twisted but normal process to judge religions, political groups, in business, or even against family members when someone wants to feel he is superior to a mate, parent, brother or sister. What makes similarities and differences powerful and potentially dangerous is that we can use this tool to justify almost any judgment, cruelty or exploitation, quickly and decisively.

One key to using similarities and differences to manipulate rather than understand requires that we *exaggerate* differences and *diminish* similarities. By contrast, to ingratiate for advantage—like when falling in love, or selling cars—the opposite is required. Now, we must *exaggerate* similarities and *ignore* differences to control the outcome.

By contrast, when we want to understand and nurture, we identify *both* similarities *and* differences with the innocent purpose of wanting to see reality accurately and use the information to feed needs and fulfill potentials. We also use similarities and differences to help men and women acknowledge each other, rather than create conflict or competition.

Understanding Men & Women

Normally, men and women assume the genders are basically different. After focusing on *differences* it has been rare for members of either gender to make a conscious effort to explore *similarities.* Since differences provide a handy basis for criticism, men and women frequently first identify a difference, and then label it *right, wrong, good, or bad.* Judging differences only adds fuel to the fire of competition and conflict, and makes it difficult to impossible for men and women to understand each other.

While it is true that men and women experience some differences in their priorities and purposes, this does not make them fundamentally different. For instance, men and women are *similar* in that both genders experience the same fundamental *facts-of-life* and *internal needs.* As a result, every man and woman is alone in his/her lifespan, and solely responsible for mastering his/her internal needs.

Of course, men and women are similar in that both suffer when they fail to complete their developmental tasks. In addition, men and women are similar in their desire to avoid pain and deny responsibility. Finally, both men and women often rely on approval for self-worth, and in spite of this dependence, both genders like to believe they are independent. Their mutual addiction to approval, however, reveals the truth.

Up to this point, we have focused primarily on the similarities between men and women. The reason is that most people can identify differences, and while they rarely understand them, they are at least familiar with their existence. While differences are neither more nor less important than similarities, we need to see that *differences* reveal what is *unique* about each gender. On the other hand, *similarities* must be seen to identify everything we *share in common*.

For example, one difference between the genders is that men, as a group, are physically larger. Women, on the other hand, are alone in becoming pregnant and bearing children. These facts illuminate two significant differences that have created dramatic consequences for both sexes.

One consequence of the fact that nature usually makes men bigger and stronger is they have used physical advantage to create social and economic advantages as well. From a position of physical dominance, men have evangelized a *belief* they were superior to women—when in fact, they were just bigger!

For their part, because they become pregnant and bear children, women have a connection to the wonder of creation and birth that men can imagine, but never experience. At the same time, because of menstruation, childbirth, and child rearing, women tend to experience a more personal and intimate connection to both pain and joy than most men.

Finally, partly because women often have sole responsibility for emotional needs, they may be more likely to value empathy and compassion. One consequence is that women often want to talk about their feelings more than men.

Can you see that if we identify differences *without* judgment we can understand what is *unique* in each gender's experience? By contrast, is it obvious that if we define differences *with* judgment, we create competition and conflict?

Unfortunately, *defining differences with judgment* has been the most common use of this tool, whether between genders, cultures, races, or human beings and nature. ***Whenever people want to feel superior or gain advantage, they only have to exaggerate a real or imaginary difference.***

Probably the only way we will use similarities and differences honestly is when we discover that we *need* understanding. Once we acknowledge that understanding is a real need, we will have a solidly selfish reason to replace judgments, beliefs, and feelings with genuine understanding.

Spiritual Leaders vs. Infamous Villains

In the next example, we will use similarities and differences to compare two of the world's greatest spiritual leaders with two of the most dangerous villains. Defining the similarities and differences between these four men, without judgment, compels our minds to observe reality from a perspective that may feel repugnant, or at least unfamiliar. At the same time, this example may increase our awareness in ways that would not seem possible at the outset.

For instance, if we observe the similarities between Jesus and Buddha on one side, and Josef Stalin and Adolph Hitler on the other, we embark on a mission that can seem impossible, and even hints at being sacrilegious. Nonetheless, let us engage this task and discover if life-affirming insights may be the consequence, and our reward, no matter how outrageous it may appear at first glance.

If we begin by observing the facts that define all four men, we lay a foundation of insight necessary to identify all the similarities and differences. For instance, both Stalin and Hitler were undisputed leaders of their respective countries. In addition, both maintained their positions for life, and both acquired the highest level of external power any human can wield. This means Stalin and Hitler organized their countries in accordance with their every whim, and had complete power over the life and death of literally everyone. This is the pinnacle of *external* power available to a human being.

By contrast, Buddha and Jesus, each in his own way, reached the pinnacle of *internal* power. Paradoxically, both the greatest Masters of internal development and the most infamous political villains reached a pinnacle of power.

To reach any pinnacle requires concentrated energy, effort, and attention over a long span of time. This means that Buddha, Jesus, Stalin, and Hitler all shared one similar characteristic; each one could concentrate effort, energy, and attention on a single purpose, and with total commitment.

This insight identifies another similarity in that all four men had clearly defined *purposes*. Following a specific purpose provided each man with a structure that established his priorities, guided every decision, and identified his critical tasks each day. In addition, all four men committed the time, effort, energy, and attention necessary to fulfill his specific purposes. This means that each man engaged his life's mission with focused attention and whole-hearted passion.

Finally, another significant similarity is that all four men accepted the fact that accomplishing his goals required standing alone and being his own authority. Hitler and Stalin could look to no one, in part because they were blazing new trails in degrees of treachery and murder literally unprecedented in human history.

On the other hand, Buddha and Jesus were also blazing new trails—only in degrees of consciousness, compassion, and understanding that were also unprecedented. ***One lesson we can learn from Buddha and Jesus is that internal development is similar to external achievement in that it requires standing alone and being our own authority.***

Another lesson we can learn from the similarities between these four men is that all extreme accomplishment, whether it results in a sublime affirmation of truth and life or a total negation of truth and destruction of life, requires a whole-hearted commitment of energy, time, effort, and attention. All extreme accomplishment also requires a commitment to clearly defined purposes.

From these similarities, we can see that the underlying *processes* necessary to be life affirming can also be used to create devastating destruction. This insight reveals that mental and emotional development cannot be compressed into simple rules, but must be understood in terms of experience, especially if we want to design a truly life affirming experience of being alive that is uniquely our own.

Once we identify the similarities, it is appropriate to acknowledge differences. For instance, one significant difference is that Stalin and Hitler achieved only *external* power, whereas Buddha and Christ developed *internal* power. No other difference is more important.

One reason this difference is significant is that external power does **not** satisfy internal needs, and is something we must lose, either because someone takes it away, as was the case for Hitler, or because we simply grow old and die, which was Stalin's fate. On the other hand, the internal power that is a result of mental and emotional development has a lasting satisfaction and meaning that lives on, even after we are gone.

We can identify another difference by observing the daily lives of Hitler and Stalin, and seeing that both men spent their days filled with fear. They were always afraid that someone would try to kill and replace them. As a result, their lives were devoid of joy, and even their pleasure was stolen from days devoted to protecting themselves while doing their best to injure others. One result of this sad process is that Adolph and Joseph lived and died frightened, paranoid, and pitifully insecure. They were always trying to project an *image* of strength in order to hide the *fact* that their minds were tormented and fearful.

Now, compare these tragic lives with the experience of Buddha and Jesus. Here, we have two men with real mental and emotional development, as defined by the fact that both men created *conscious and life-affirming purposes,* and clearly valued *thinking for understanding.*

As a result, the days of Buddha and Jesus were spent pursuing truth and feeding needs, while also fulfilling every internal potential. This means that instead of being insecure, both men fully mastered peace of mind. In addition, rather than being fearful, we see two minds motivated by the love of truth. Finally, instead of being dedicated to destruction, we see two men committed to understanding and nurturing life in the form of teaching compassion and internal competence.

The consequences of these two vastly different responses to being alive are extreme. From Stalin and Hitler, we see painful consequences that span a generation or two, but ultimately, like all destructiveness simply dissolve into the sands of time and are lost from memory. Like all the great villains whose only legacy was some form of destruction—Stalin and Hitler too, will disappear forever.

Buddha and Jesus, however, created new levels of awareness, and their lives will always be a clear reflection of two beings innocently developing consciousness and caring. Their legacies will be inspiring and relevant for as long as anyone struggles to develop his mind and emotions, or strives to live consciously and with meaning.

Applying the Lessons

The purpose of identifying similarities and differences between famous people now long dead is to introduce this mental tool in a way that I hope will not be too threatening. If this is the case, try asking questions about your own life, such as, "Have I consciously defined my purposes?" Then, "What seems more important to me, *internal or external* achievement?" Finally, "Am I working to expand my understanding and internal competence, or do I leave in my life's wake a trail of self-absorption and internal emptiness?"

These questions are useful for exploring and learning, so *consciously* ask and answer each question and note whether you *work to understand*—or unconsciously *judge*? This is important, because if you do **not** judge you can learn from defining the choices you have made, and the consequences you created.

You can also study the lives of Buddha, Jesus, Hitler, and Stalin to see their choices and the consequences they created. Once you understand the choices, purposes, and consequences that define all four lives, you can use this information to compare with the choices *you* make, and the consequences *you* create. If you can do this without judging, you imitate the wisdom of Buddha and Jesus. However, if you feel compelled to judge, then you imitate the attitudes of Stalin and Hitler, who were masters at using judgments to manipulate and distort reality.

Finally, if you can use similarities and differences to understand the greatest spiritual masters in contrast to the worst political villains, you can do the same between yourself and other people. For instance, whenever you experience conflict with a mate, child, friend, stranger, or business associate, begin by exploring your similarities and you will have a much greater chance of resolving the conflict.

Following a conscious process where you purposefully look for similarities with an innocent desire to understand, is opposite to a normal process where you unconsciously identify differences so you can justify judging and arguing.

This means that if you want to resolve painful situations, you must identify similarities even if you "feel" certain the other person is so "bad" that you could not share anything. Identifying similarities builds bridges to other people, in part because they create empathy and agreement. No other insight is as critical in learning how to resolve conflict. If you identify similarities that create points of empathy and agreement, then by the time you define differences you will have established an *attitude* of cooperation that encourages understanding, so conflicts can actually be resolved.

Describing the Content Of Each Experience

From our first gasp of surprise at being born to the last sigh of our final surrender, one event follows another in an unbroken progression. You can easily observe this process by watching how external facts and actions, along with internal thoughts and emotions, all continue to tumble one after another every moment of your existence.

One way to organize the chaotic events of being alive is to observe the *facts, your responses, and the consequences* to help identify the details of each experience. For example, if in *fact* you have time to fill, and then *respond* by watching a movie, there are *consequences.* If you observe this sequence accurately and without judgment, you will see the *content* of this one experience.

With normal training, people rarely define the content of any experience. Instead, they don't even notice everyday *facts, their responses, and the consequences* unless some degree of dramatic pain or pleasure is involved. Even then, people tend to view consequences as a punishment or reward, and fail to observe and learn from ordinary experience.

For example, if an event is painful we normally react with a simplistic, "Hell, that hurt! I'm not going to do that again!" By contrast, if an experience is pleasurable we say, "Hey that was great, let's do it again!" With either response, we *react* to the moment without first just describing in detail what happened. Of course, no one would think to identify their responses and define the consequences. Instead, all we normally acknowledge is that we experienced pleasure and want to do it again, or were dismayed that the experience was unpleasant or painful and want to avoid repeating it.

Exploring Experience

The inability to describe and learn from daily experience results in stumbling through existence *reacting* to pleasure and pain, but never *understanding* precisely what is true, or clearly defining our needs and potentials. One consequence is that we rarely acknowledge the present, fail to understand the past, and have no purpose or plan for the future.

What this insight teaches is that if you want to grow wise—not just old—then you must learn to observe facts, explore them with questions, and discover what is true and needed.

You can observe the need to explore experience every day. For example, if you want to discover what is required to make human life satisfying and meaningful, *observe* the content of other people's lives until you see the critical facts in each person's life. Next, *explore* each person's responses. Finally, *discover* the specific responses that created satisfying *consequences*—and those that did not.

If you want to describe the content of your own life, stop and ask, "What in fact do I think about each day?" and, "How do I spend my time and energy? What are the consequences? Are my days satisfying and meaningful, empty and painful, or just mindlessly pleasant?"

Normally, people are so busy reacting to pain, pleasure, and the demands of daily life they are unaware of the content of their experience. In fact, we often so overfill each day with tasks and distractions that life is a blur of activity. One natural consequence is that we do not leave enough time or energy to become aware we are even alive. Since self-induced oblivion is normal the *content* of daily life is often invisible, so we seldom notice the details, like whether or not we are consciously content and internally fulfilled!

Of course, the facts that affect other people—like whether our children develop self-worth or our mates are internally satisfied—are beyond the scope of our normal minds. We simply never notice whether we have fulfilled our potential to be a competent parent, satisfying mate, or real friend.

It is important to observe that everyone needs to master observing, exploring, discovering and changing just to see the *content* of everyday life, which to a mind with normal training is largely invisible. Learning how to accurately describe content provides the basic information crucial to master the next and last mental tool, *Understanding Process.*

Understanding Process

You have just seen that *describing content* defines "what happened". Next, to explore the *meaning* of what happened, we must identify *process,* which we can define as the *invisible patterns hiding inside the content.* To identify our internal processes, we need to observe daily experience until we see repeated patterns in our attitudes, purposes, needs, choices and behaviors.

For example, if you walk down a sidewalk and stumble on a hose lying across your path, one response is to exclaim, "That damn hose tripped me!" You could also blame an unknown person, "Who was the unconscious slob who left this hose here!" On the other hand, you could honestly admit, "I wasn't paying attention and I tripped over the hose."

In another example, imagine that your mate has decided to leave you for another person. A *normal* response might be, "After all the years that I *gave* so much and *asked* so little, and now, my ungrateful mate has abandoned me!" Or, you could respond *consciously,* "It has been a long time since I gave my mate whole-hearted energy and attention, and I never did offer a personal conversation or conscious touch, so now I am paying the price for my lack of caring, skill, and attention". You could also add, "I can understand that my mate would want to be with someone who at least seems to care more than I have, or in fact offers a satisfying experience of giving, growing, and sharing."

Identifying Patterns

If you want to understand *process,* then you must see the universal *patterns* hiding inside these two unique situations. Process reveals the predictable attitudes and behaviors that a person consistently expresses toward the facts of experience. For instance, in the first example a normal person first responds with anger and then *blames* the hose as well as some unknown person for creating the unexpected experience of tripping. By contrast, the conscious person is relaxed and accepts sole *responsibility* for the experience.

In the next example, the normal person reacts by feeling hurt and angry—then justifies himself and blames his mate. In stark contrast, the conscious person responds by first trying to understand what happened, and then acknowledges his own role and responsibility in this very painful event.

With normal training, our predictable reaction to painful events is to justify ourselves and blame someone else. Justifying and blaming are *normal processes* that we repeat in every situation where we feel threatened—or experience pain, failure, or loss.

On the other hand, with a *conscious process* we learn to respond to unexpected or painful facts by first describing what happened, and then we take responsibility for our part. With a *conscious process* we want to understand everyone's perspective, and never even want to blame someone for our inadequacies, or inanimate objects for our lack of attention.

We develop wisdom by first describing the content of each significant experience and then clearly identify the critical patterns and processes hiding inside. Mastering the ability to *describe content* and *understand process* is necessary to learn about ourselves, life, and other people.

In science, we have seen that observable *laws of nature* create objective *processes* that govern the physical world. For instance, gravity on planet earth is a perfectly predictable phenomenon. As a result, we can predict with perfect certainty that anyone who jumps off a building is going to hit the ground. Of course, we cannot predict whether the fall will kill or injure them. This only means that our predictive power is limited, even when we understand process.

In spite of its limits, the mental tool of understanding process is essential for acquiring layer upon layer of insight. Scientists know that defining process is a pre-requisite to understanding the physical world, but as a group, people have failed to use this tool to understand themselves.

Instead, rather than observe ourselves with the purpose of understanding the processes critical to expressing love and developing wisdom, we learn to value status quo over change, and beliefs and feelings over facts. One consequence of acquiring these *normal processes* is that we never learn how to think for understanding, or care with a whole heart. ***As a result, following normal mental processes makes it almost as certain that we will create a disconnected and unfulfilled life as the physical process of gravity insures that if we jump off a building we will fall to the ground.***

Happiness & Caring

We have seen that normal processes make internal growth not just difficult, but impossible. Of course, if someone does not ***care*** about creating internal development and/or happiness, this limitation will not matter. It is important to notice that what you fail to care about receives no energy. Consequently, if you do not care about internal fulfillment, you will not want mental and emotional training. Caring is critical.

All adults have an option whether or not to care about their own internal needs and enduring happiness. For instance, *caring* about truth and beauty is optional. However, we *need* to experience both, and if we fail to feed these needs then we experience some degree of damage to our internal fulfillment. The lesson here is that if you want to be happy, you must ***care about and want what you need.***

Caring about and wanting what you need establishes a *conscious process* that helps you become consistent in making life-affirming choices. It also takes you a step away from being normal. Taking a step away from the herd—even a life-affirming step—can be frightening. This is why moving away from the normal processes can feel risky, frightening, exhilarating—or even all three at the same time!

Happiness & Exploring

If you want to create internal happiness, thinking for understanding is an essential *process*. For one, you need to think about daily events to identify the invisible patterns in your responses to pain, risk, and all real needs. Once you clearly see the *processes* that define your attitudes, purposes, and responses, you can *stay the course* and maintain your status quo, or *change your process*.

To identify your processes, observe how you respond to life's large issues like choosing a career or mate, as well as the everyday choices in how to spend time, or whether to feed your mind truth and emotions beauty. Identifying the attitudes and purposes responsible for every choice is significant because these *processes* define the content of your life, and are often invisible to a mind with normal training.

The great masters of human life knew that understanding process is critical to becoming wise. Their response was to observe, ask questions, and explore life until they *understood* their own attitudes, purposes, needs, and potentials, as well those of other people and Nature. As a result, the great masters were conscious, caring, and competent to a degree that for normal minds often seems mystical, or supernatural.

By contrast, ***normal minds often remain primitive, in part, because a "normal process" demands that we look for "simple answers to complex realities"***. The field of nutrition provides a modern example of how silly we can become in our search for simple answers. For instance, years ago, when margarine first came on the market, cost was the primary issue and people thought margarine was an inferior substitute for butter. Then, *studies showed* that butter is *bad,* but margarine is *good!* In recent years, *new studies* show that butter is *good* and margarine is *bad*. We have repeated a similar process with eggs, cheese, milk, sugar, and fats.

In each case, some study offers a simplistic solution to a complex problem. The real issue is that becoming healthy by eating well is a complex process that cannot be reduced to a simple solution to fit our one-dimensional mentality. This means that if you want to be physically healthy—or if you want the internal experience of genuine joy, internal happiness, and real meaning—then you must master the awareness and skills required for internal development.

One reason human beings have not formally taught wisdom is that it requires mastering multiple complex processes—i.e. feeding needs and fulfilling potentials, as well as thinking for understanding and building emotional bonds—which are all necessary for internal development.

It is not a surprise that with this pre-requisite, and no immediately obvious external reward, few human beings *consciously* pursue the internal development necessary to become loving and wise. Instead, people unconsciously pursue *normal* priorities they hope will result in getting approval, pleasure, or security.

Unfortunately, what everyday experience reveals is that the excitement of pleasure, approval, and security is temporary, while feelings of emptiness and futility are durable, and eventually or even quickly, come screaming back!

By the time we learn this tragic lesson it is often too late, either because too much of our life has passed, or because we identify with *normal processes* too thoroughly to change. One sad consequence is that human beings are in some ways as unconscious and emotionally primitive now, as when we lived in caves and drew pictures of animals on the walls.

Everyone needs to see and understand the processes necessary to develop the *consciousness, caring, and internal competence* that creates wisdom, love, and internal fulfillment. If you want wisdom, then you must master all the mental tools. Next, you need to apply the mental tools toward building a complete inventory of insight. It is important to notice that *complete* does not mean you have to understand everything. It only means that you master internal needs and potentials, thinking for understanding, and caring wholeheartedly.

If you master these developmental tasks, then when it comes time to die you will experience no regret, fear, or hanging-on. Instead, having become consciously content and internally fulfilled, you will fall gently from the tree of life like a piece of ripe fruit.

Mastering the ability to live with enduring satisfaction and true meaning—and dying fulfilled and complete—are internal rewards for mental and emotional development. These rewards are largely invisible to a normally trained mind following normal purposes and processes. Here, in this book is a life-affirming *conscious alternative* to the normal purpose and process. Hopefully, you will find it both comforting and challenging to have a real alternative and genuine choice. Now, it's time to choose.

PART IV:

Building Bonded Relationships

Building Bonded Relationships
Introduction & Overview

Everyone experiences a real and innocent need for emotionally bonded relationships. In spite of the fact that every person experiences this need—and that human beings have had thousands of years to work on it—observing everyday life quickly reveals that people have failed to define, in detail, *how* to build bonded relationships. The primary reason for this perplexing oversight has been normal training.

As we have seen, people normally adopt ideas and beliefs, or follow their feelings while trying to fit in with the social forms that define what is good, bad, right, and wrong. Consequently, people choose a mate or create a family with no training in how to define and feed a single internal need. *Impersonal* and unsatisfying relationships are inevitable.

Building bonded relationships is a complex activity that surprisingly, begins by acknowledging that as far as anyone can observe—*life is a mystery, and death is forever.* Accepting this reality is critical to emotional bonding because it identifies the fundamental human predicament that everyone experiences. If you *consciously acknowledge* that life is a mystery and death is forever, then you identify a frightening reality that you share in common with every other human being—as well as every bird, animal, fish, plant or tree on the planet.

Consciously sharing inescapable facts that define critical elements in everyone's life builds a bridge to other people, and opens the door to comforting one another through *personal conversation*. In contrast, the normal reaction to life's frightening facts is to deny or explain them away. This distorts reality, and when we try to form relationships based on distortions we can never build genuine emotional bonds.

One reason is that emotional bonds require a foundation based on innocently and honestly acknowledging the facts. ***If we are dishonest about the fundamental facts of life, then we build relationships on the "sands of deception" rather than the "rock of reality".*** Neither a relationship nor an individual can grow when fed with distortions and deceptions.

This may present a problem for people who want to build their lives and relationships on being honest, and yet, want to integrate religious, philosophical, or spiritual beliefs. To do both simply requires acknowledging that ideas, faiths, and beliefs—whatever else they are—are not facts. If you think about it, every *belief* is a *hope* that something is true. This means all beliefs and faiths are similar in that none can be proven true or false. Every faith, no matter how old or new, is a personal opinion and a subjective choice.

Conversely, objective observations define facts of reality that you can confirm are true, and share with other people. This means you can *believe* in a religion, philosophy, or spiritual practice, and still acknowledge that as far as anyone has been able to observe, *life is a mystery and death is forever.* With this honest acknowledgment, you can share *observable facts,* while also retaining your *beliefs* and never distort reality or create prejudice to protect your mental status quo.

Giving Interest & Sharing Reality

Consciously sharing the basic facts that define human life is one emotional comfort that we can give to one another. Giving and receiving comfort is a basic building block for all emotional bonds. If you want to grow in your ability to give and share the attitudes of *curiosity, innocence, and responsibility* are critical. For instance, you need *innocence* and *curiosity* to be genuinely interested in other people. Of course, as we have seen *whole-hearted interest* is something everyone needs.

It is a paradox that every person is hungry for interest, but almost no one can ask even a single intelligent question, wait attentively for the answer, and then ask another intelligent question with the conscious purpose of wanting to understand someone else's experience and perspective. The problem is that to express real interest in another person, we must first master thinking for understanding, caring whole-heartedly, and feeding internal needs for ourselves.

Without satisfying these pre-requisites, we do not have the internal development necessary to forget ourselves and be truly interested in someone else. This illuminates one reason that genuine emotional bonds are rare—that is, while everyone is hungry for interest and attention, almost no one is internally developed enough to offer it. Consequently, when people choose a mate or become parents the normal purpose is to *get* interest and attention, **not** *give* it.

In the world of normal relationships everyone is quick to evaluate what he is *getting*, but slow to observe what he/she is *giving*. If you want to build bonded relationships you must do the opposite of normal and *observe, define,* and *improve* the quality of interest and attention that you *give*. You also never criticize someone else for a lack of attention and interest. This is a simple prescription, but without internal development it is impossible to understand and apply.

Building bonded relationships begins with *observing* and *sharing reality*. Next, you need to master *giving energy* and *attention* as part of offering *personal conversation* and *conscious touch*. To create a lifetime of internal growth, you and your mate also need to define and share *conscious purposes, primal experience and quintessential moments.* All five elements are necessary to maintain and expand emotional bonds.

Raising the "Ceiling of Expectations"

Consciously mastering each step in building bonded relationships requires taking a jackhammer to the cement ceiling of low expectations that constricts most normal minds and emotions.

In normal life, our primary purpose is to control approval and security, so our highest goal is often to just make daily life as pleasant and comfortable as possible. Frequently, we do not even hope for a life of mental and emotional risk, challenge, and change. Nor do we expect to love with a whole heart, or to pursue understanding until we go where "no person has gone before!" Nor do we expect to experience beauty with an intensity that makes our bodies ache with the joy and pain of it. Instead, we pursue lives of bland comfort and monotonous security, and then justify the internal emptiness by saying: "It's more than most people have!" and add, "I don't want much; I just want to be happy." Oh Joy! Or just a long yawn?

Raising the *ceiling of low expectations* changes everything. First, you expect to work every day of your life. However, instead of working to get security and approval, you work to understand the mystery of being alive. This includes the *universal* developmental tasks as well as the hopes, talents and dreams that define your *unique* potentials. In addition, you *expect* to acknowledge and understand your mate, children, and friends. Eventually, you *expect* to understand every person on the planet—and finally—every animal, bird, fish, plant, and tree. Bugs are optional.

With normal training, we do not even aspire to understand ourselves, much less other people. Consequently, rather than learn how to understand and nurture—we learn to *compete* and *exploit*. We need to observe that relationships based on *competition* and *exploitation* can never build emotional bonds. Instead, genuine emotional bonds require mastering *five internal needs.*

Internal Needs Necessary to Build Emotional Bonds

- **Personal Conversation**
- **Conscious Touch**
- **Share—Reality, Purposes, & Quintessential Moments**

Equality and Reciprocity

It is exciting to know that if you master these five needs, then you will be prepared to *offer* a genuine emotional bond. Of course, *building a bonded romantic relationship* requires two people who are equal and reciprocal in awareness and skill. *Equality and reciprocity* are required for long-term satisfaction, internal growth, and meaning in all *adult* relationships: whether with a mate, friend, or business associate.

In the next three chapters we will define the internal needs essential for creating intimacy. As you read, memorize the ideas and then apply the information to everyday experience until you develop the awareness and skills necessary to create intimacy in every important relationship.

Personal Conversation

The oldest internal hunger, and one that all human beings share in common, is a need to experience *personal conversations* with our parents. Since few parents receive training in how to feed this universal need, most people remain forever hungry. Nonetheless, we all need parents who can ***give*** *energy and attention*, ***select*** *meaningful topics*, ***explore*** the topic in detail, and help us ***discover*** *ourselves, life, and other people.* If our parents fail to teach us, we must provide for ourselves.

Personal conversation is necessary to see ourselves accurately, define internal needs, and learn how to think and care. The intimacy created by *personal* conversation contrasts sharply with the distance produced by the *impersonal* nature of most normal conversation. For instance, in a typical parent/child conversation the primary focus is on the parent's judgments, beliefs, and feelings—rather than the child's needs, experiences, and potentials. One consequence is that most children understand their parents' perspectives far better than vice versa.

In fact, rather than teach our children how to use conversation to *explore* experience for the purpose of understanding, we usually teach them—unconsciously and by example rather than by design—how to use conversation to *get* attention and approval, to distort reality, or to manipulate outcomes.

Normal vs. Conscious Purposes

Sadly, *normal purposes* provide the primary underlying motivation for most conversations. To confirm this insight, observe yourself and other people in ordinary conversation. Do you see people listening with whole-hearted attention, while also asking questions in a context of innocent warmth and genuine interest? Next, do you see people initiate conversation with the *purpose* of sharing and understanding everyday experience—the positive and negative, beautiful and ugly, inspiring and depressing?

Or, do you find that normal conversations are often defined by a desire to ***get*** attention, talk trivia, or mindlessly express judgmental opinions, feelings, and beliefs? Normal conversation may even be a childlike competition for *airtime.* Predictably, no one wins this competition. Instead, everyone comes away frustrated and hungry, and generally confused about how the conversation could be so unsatisfying.

Nowhere is frustration and hunger more easily observed than in romantic relationships. Here, people depend upon each other for satisfying personal conversations, but normal purposes keep the topics impersonal, repetitive, or trivial. Nothing so kills passion as knowing you can predict with perfect certainty that conversation with your mate will be impersonal, superficial, or simply repetitive.

By contrast, with internal development, you adopt a *conscious purpose* to use conversation to create intimacy. Now, instead of trying to get energy and approval, talk trivia, or express judgments, you learn to acknowledge the *facts* of another person's experience, their *responses,* and the *consequences*. On the other hand, if someone asks about your life, you take the time and give the energy required to articulate significant experiences, thoughts, and feelings. This means that whether listening or talking, your purpose is to *share and understand* the entire gamut of experiences that life provides.

Thinking & Caring

Is it apparent that giving conscious thought and whole-hearted caring to both listening and talking will improve the degree of satisfaction and meaning you derive from daily conversations?

For contrast, ask a normal person whether they both listen and talk with a focused mind and whole-hearted caring. A typical answer is "No." This reveals that people are often too hungry to *get* undivided attention and interest to ever *give* it. Also, with normal training, many people never learn how to focus their minds long enough to clearly define a meaningful topic or identifiable point. As a result, few people can distinguish between a *meaningful conversation* that explores a *significant subject*—and *self-absorbed babbling*. Instead, people often free-associate in the hope that a meaningful topic or significant point will somehow just appear.

What we learn from listening to normal conversation is that people often express and *re-express* sentimental feelings, judgmental beliefs, or favorite clichés and silly sayings. Regurgitating our favorite mental tapes makes normal conversation predictably impersonal. In trying to be polite, however, we sometimes allow the other person time to express their judgments, clichés, and painfully silly sayings.

After a lifetime of swapping monologues, most people are desperately hungry for personal conversation. The problem is that until we experience a contrast—***a conversation begun with a meaningful topic, guided by conscious thought, offered with real warmth and true interest, and expanded by intelligent questions***—we have no model for offering personal conversation.

What everyone needs is a detailed model, so he can create conversations that are personal, satisfying, and meaningful. The following *requirements* for personal conversation provide the necessary model.

Three Requirements

- **Identify a Meaningful Topic**
- **Explore the Topic in Detail**
- **Understand Someone's Experience or Perspective**

The first step in offering a conversation that will create a personal connection between you and another person is to identify a *meaningful topic*. Harder than it might seem, selecting a significant topic is critical. To begin, it is important to notice that any topic has meaning if someone ***cares*** about it. No caring—no meaning! Even survival has no meaning to someone who does not care about it. So, try to observe what people care about, and if you cannot see what someone cares about—ask him in a manner that reveals your genuine interest in understanding his perspective.

The next step in selecting a meaningful topic is to separate topics into *external* and *internal*. External topics are easy to identify. For instance, men are often interested in their work, sports, travel, TV, or a whole gamut of adult male toys, i.e. cars, trucks, electronic gadgets, etc. Females too, have a typical list of external topics that are favorite sources of conversation that include but are not limited to work, shopping, clothes, children, men, house decorating, etc. Most people talk about *external* topics more comfortably than *internal* topics. As a result, cocktail conversation and party chatter is usually restricted to trivial external topics that have no real meaning in anyone's life.

Since *internal* topics are more difficult to identify and define than *external*, they require more skill and attention. This is one reason that many people never discuss a single internal topic with anyone close to them. Remember ***"internal" is defined as anything involving your mind and emotions***. This means that thoughts and emotions, as well as mental and emotional needs, potentials, desires, pains, hungers and fulfillments, are all *internal* experiences.

For instance, a man can talk endlessly about a favorite spectator sport, the players involved, their stats, close games, etc. and feel *gratified* by the experience. However, the conversation never becomes *personal* until he acknowledges an internal issue, like what this game *means* to him.

How does someone know what something *means* to him? Well, we can ask a man how much time he spends watching his favorite sport and measure his commitment, in part, by the sheer quantity of lifetime he devotes to being a spectator. Next, we can ask him what this activity provides. For instance, in detail, how does this activity enhance his life? On the other hand, does he ever feel that he loses something because of his involvement? If so, what does he lose?

These questions help us define the *internal meaning* of an *external activity*, which is one way to make a conversation *personal*.

Most people are involved in, and to a degree care about, some *external* activity or pursuit. In addition, most people are comfortable talking about the superficial details of an external pursuit, so choosing to talk about the details of someone's external pursuits is usually a *safe* subject, and as we have seen, safe external topics provide the grist for most party chatter and cocktail conversation.

Unfortunately, superficial topics provide too much of the grist for conversation between romantic partners, parents and children, and lifelong friends. Of course, meaning comes in layers, so if someone shows real interest in hearing about our hobbies, pastimes or superficial obsessions—and we get to talk at some length—most of us will feel that the conversation was *gratifying*. Trivial topics may be pleasant, but they are at the bottom of the meaning ladder, and while party chatter may gratify our *desire* for attention, it cannot feed our *need* to experience a *personal* connection to life and other people.

Exploring Issues

Anytime you want to elevate normal party chatter to something personal then *explore* an external topic by asking what the activity or pursuit requires, and provides. For instance, "What does the activity add to someone's experience of being alive? What does it cost in terms of time and effort? What makes the activity worth the time and effort it costs?" Of course, you must ask these questions in a relaxed tone motivated by innocent interest, and never in the tense tone or aggressive delivery of a judgmental district attorney!

Another path for selecting and exploring meaningful topics is to first identify significant *facts* in another person's life, and then ask *intelligent questions* that explore the internal and external details. For example, say a friend is struggling to find a job that will not only pay the bills, but will also be mentally and emotionally challenging and meaningful. Asking your friend what he cares about, has to offer, and how he feels about waiting, struggling, and maybe even suffering in order to get a meaningful job opens a personal discussion.

You can also ask your friend about interviewing strategies. For instance, how will he describe his desire for the job, or his competence to do the tasks? Finally, you could ask your friend to identify his greatest fears and insecurities, and how he responds to each one.

The purpose of personal conversation is to offer *energy and interest* and *explore* another person's experience, thought, and emotion. ***This means you must want to learn, share, and understand, not solve problems and offer advice.*** A conscious purpose to understand is critical. Normally, if we cannot solve someone's problems, we do not want to hear about his issues. Instead, we often *pretend interest,* which becomes evident when we respond to a crucial moment in someone's life with no more depth or exploration than a newspaper headline.

Point of Understanding

Another way to distinguish *personal* from *normal* conversation is to observe that in *normal conversation* a topic is often limited to a sentence or two, but in a *personal conversation* we *explore* a topic to the *point of understanding.* For instance, understanding someone requires that we explore and define his purposes, motivations, needs, choices, and behaviors.

The purpose for personal conversation is one: To feed another person's need for interest and attention; and two: to explore a meaningful topic until we understand some part of the other person's experience or perspective.

You can practice *personal conversation* when your mate complains that you do not *give* enough—like not enough time or attention. A normal response is to deny that the complaint is valid, or justify and explain the neglect. By contrast, a *conscious response* confirms your mate's reality by looking for a *grain of truth.* In this case, you acknowledge that the quality or quantity of your attention is partially, or even completely inadequate. Then, you willingly *explore* the topic by asking intelligent questions.

When you explore issues wanting to understand, and neither point nor avoid the fickle finger of blame, you discover what is true and define what is needed. Following this process you can transform a *negative complaint* into *positive understanding*, which will feed your mate's internal need and contribute to building a genuine emotional bond.

The Grain of Truth

Essential to understanding anything is to always look for a *grain of truth,* even if someone is critical and what he says is painful to hear. If you look for the *grain of truth* you build trust, which means the other person will feel safe to be honest and vulnerable *trusting* that the conversation will be productive and result in understanding rather than irresolvable conflict.

In stark contrast, with normal training people invariably look for the *grain of error* in what another person says, especially when he/she is complaining or being critical. In looking for the *grain of error* a normal response to complaints or criticisms is often, "Well, that's not *entirely* true!" or my personal favorite, "That is not 100% true." Then, we pick apart the complaint or criticism and make it seem as if there is *no truth* in what the person is saying. This process is unsatisfying, in part because the relevant issues are never defined or explored. Since normal conversation is what most people offer and receive, we rarely trust that talking will create understanding or resolve conflict.

At the heart of every conversation is a *process*. For example, following a *normal process* people make all the usual choices to avoid pain, distort reality, get attention, and go for simple answers. One consequence is that normal conversations are often self-absorbed, one-dimensional, predictable, and hopelessly competitive. On the other hand, in adopting a *conscious process* it is our *purpose* to acknowledge facts, give attention, and pursue understanding.

Conversation is the cornerstone for building bonded relationships because it is the single most powerful source for sharing experience and understanding perspective. On the negative side, it can also be the most powerful instrument for creating distance, conflict, and isolation.

The problem, of course, is that no one can learn a technique and become competent to offer personal conversation. Instead, each person must acquire all the awareness and skills necessary to master internal needs and potentials, think for understanding and care whole-heartedly. Without the internal foundation provided by mental and emotional development, no one can offer a truly personal conversation, or build a genuine emotional bond.

Conscious Touch

In addition to the need for *personal conversation*, everyone needs *conscious touch*. While most people can acknowledge a desire for a warm hug, or for someone to hold their hand or put an arm around their waist or over their shoulder, rarely does anyone distinguish between a *conscious touch* and the *unconscious pat, peck, or whack* that often defines the normal experience. There is in fact, a world of difference.

What are the differences between a normal pat, peck or whack, and a conscious touch? To begin, the motivation and purpose for a conscious touch are different, as is the degree of awareness, skill, and sensual sensitivity that directs the behavior. Other than that, they are about the same.

The purpose for a normal touch is to get something. The normal purpose of wanting to manipulate for energy and approval is certainly a common reason for touching, but a desire for pleasure is also normal. Sometimes, people touch to create sentimental feelings, or gain advantage, but there is usually no *conscious purpose* to share and nurture.

The normal motivation to touch comes from a *reaction* to feeling lonely, or internally empty. One consequence is that normal touching is often motivated by a reactive desire to feel good, rather than a *conscious* desire to nurture and share. Sometimes, when people are impersonally touched they may feel an obligation to be polite and accept it, or react by trying to offer comfort, but no one ever feels satisfied, or experiences intimacy from an unconscious and impersonal touch.

Part of the difficulty in describing a conscious touch is that in the normal world almost every interaction is to some degree impersonal or manipulative. This is a problem because many people have no experience with being *innocent* and *conscious*. Nonetheless, we will explore the requirements for offering a conscious touch, and see what we can learn.

Basic Requirements

To begin, everyone experiences an internal need to *feel desirable*. A *conscious touch* innocently offered and backed-up by a purpose to nurture shows another person that we truly like him/her. The experience of an innocent and conscious touch provides a genuinely satisfying acknowledgment that will feed anyone's need to feel nurtured, desirable, and safe.

Of course, we must discriminate between the *filling-up* that a normal person pursues in touching to get approval, security, or pleasure, and the *innocent delight* that a conscious adult experiences in using touch to nurture internal needs.

Children and animals intuitively respond to the difference between a conscious adult who feeds their internal need, and the normal *unconscious* adult who uses the child or animal to feed himself. If there is a choice, both animals and children will move toward the conscious adult who *innocently* feeds them, and away from the normal adult who *unconsciously* exploits them. If they do not have a choice, then both children and animals will feel tense and/or anxious.

Story of the First Kiss

Conscious touch between adults is just as important as between parents and children, and the problems are similar. To understand the importance of touch in romantic relationships try to imagine how a primitive couple may have discovered the satisfying effects of touching lips, what today we call kissing. Imagine a tribe of cave-dwelling people sitting around a fire on a long summer evening. While no one is married, everyone seems coupled-up, and one of the younger and more aware of the primitive males is looking carefully at his woman. His eyes are clear, and reveal a focused but innocent interest as he studies her thoughtfully.

The two have been a couple for some time, and he is growing weary, not of her, but of the impersonal nature of their relationship. He relates to her as a normal primitive, which means that he hunts while she cooks and tidies up the cave. Whenever he feels the urge, he mounts her for his pleasure or comfort. One thing he has noticed, however, is that she does not seem to experience the pleasure or comfort from this activity that he does.

Now, he looks at her and notices that the skin around her nipples is similar in color and texture to the skin of her lips. A plastic surgeon would make a similar observation a few thousand years later, which was helpful in learning how to construct new lips from skin around the nipple. Our primitive man is just noticing a fact.

As he contemplates his newfound insight about skin, the young man searches his memory until he brings up scenes where he noticed that his woman's nipples are sensitive to heat, cold, and touch. Since the skin of his woman's lips and nipples appear similar, he begins to wonder if his lips too, are sensitive. Now, he contemplates himself, touches his own lips and notices that yes, his lips are sensitive, and seem connected to the breath that sustains his life, and his brain, which contains his unique thoughts, memories, and feelings.

Next, with these insights neatly tucked away, our young primitive again focuses attention on his woman. He begins to wonder if touching lips and sharing each other's breath might create a sensuously *personal* connection with a woman he cares about, but has not had the internal development or skill to touch in a truly meaningful way.

With a question in his mind, and an eager fearlessness in his eyes, our brave young man steps across the fire and sits next to his woman. He sees in her eyes a little apprehension from sensing something unfamiliar is coming her way, so he quiets her anxiety with a gentle touch on her arm. Then, with his eyes lightly holding hers, he slowly moves his lips toward hers until they meet.

What an unfamiliar, but utterly sweet sensation! She too is shocked, and pleased, and filled with a strange longing. Finally, an *old hunger* is satisfied, one she never knew existed—an *internal* hunger for an intensely personal experience with a man she genuinely likes and respects. She could never have fed this hunger without the satisfying experience provided by *consciously* touching lips.

Over time, our primitive couple experiments with touching lips until they learn how to put the thought and caring in their minds into touching their lips. Sometimes, they lightly brush their lips together to experience the delight of sensitive skin, and sometimes they press their lips tightly together and take in the sweet scent of each other's breath. Occasionally, they remain utterly still until they feel the life burning inside each other's lips, and for a moment, share the wonder and mystery of just being alive.

In following what happened after our young couple discovered kissing, we see a strange consequence. While washing skins down at the stream, our young woman spoke with the other women about her experience of touching lips, how personal and satisfying the experience was for her. She was excited about the warmth and intimacy created by kissing—and the changes in how she and her young man relate. The other women were also intrigued, and back in the cave demanded their pre-verbal mates learn how to touch lips too.

Under duress, the other cave men tried to do the touching lips thing. It did not have the same effect. Instead, several women experienced chipped front teeth, generally complained about their mate's awful breath, and looked back on impersonal coupling as the *good old days*!

Perhaps this story will make it obvious that conscious touching requires intelligent thought, genuine caring, and practice. It also requires an innocent motivation that cannot be controlled or manipulated. Instead, *innocent* desire is always out of control, and never diminished or twisted by *lust* for approval, pleasure, or security.

Old Hungers & New Longings

We all need conscious touching that is innocently motivated. The experience of conscious touching feeds internal hungers necessary to build genuine emotional bonds with other people. One consequence of feeding internal hungers is the ***experience** of innocent delight and genuine intimacy*. Of course, once we feed ***old hungers*** for personal conversation and conscious touch, then we also awaken ***new longings***.

For instance, where once we unconsciously accepted a daily repetition of impersonal and unconscious interactions, we now experience strong longings to give and receive only personal conversation and conscious touching. Everything else becomes a painful and frustrating waste of time.

To offer a conscious contrast to normal experience, I wrote the poem on the next page to paint a word picture of a common experience between an ordinary man and woman. Read the poem and notice whether the words awaken old hungers or new longings. Also, notice your response: do you feel relaxed, tense, or neutral—sad, glad, drained, or energized?

To an Ordinary Woman

Stepping Out of the Shower
On a Tuesday Morning
Wrapped only in a Towel

I Look at You and see Bare Shoulders
Wet Hair, and Shining Blue Eyes

I Step Forward
And take Your Head in my Two Hands
See the Depth of Longing in Your Eyes
And let the Hunger in My Lips
Meet the Warm Response in Yours!

Then, As Your Body melts into Mine
With one arm I pull You Tightly Close

Now, I Kiss You Again
This Time with a Timeless Passion
That fills Your Mind and Body with Emotion
That you feel from the Top of Your Head
To the Soles of Your Feet
And Back Again!

Through it All, I Wrap Us Both
In the Protective Light
Of My Consciousness and Caring
Searing the Moment in Both Our Memories
For All Eternity

Does it seem that the experience described in this poem would feed your hunger to be touched in a context of innocent consciousness and caring? In fact, the interactions described in this poem acknowledge and feed internal hungers basic to every man and woman.

For example, in feeding internal hungers there is always a need for awareness and restraint. Awareness is required just to experience internal needs. Restraint is needed so that both people have time to consciously receive the experience, and then honestly respond. In this case, the man looks at the woman, sees her in physical detail, steps forward and takes her head in his hands, looks into her eyes, and gives her time to respond, which she does with a look that expresses her own longing. Only then does he act, fully aware that she is present and experiencing a similar hunger.

Now, again with restraint, the ordinary man waits until the woman responds to his kiss, and then with awareness and passion pulls her close. At this point, the actions and responses of both people are blending and swelling like a wave that begins growing far out to sea and continues to gather strength and momentum as it comes closer to the shore. Being aware of the connection between internal hunger and external action, the ordinary man understands the power of a conscious touch and kiss, and the passionate response that it will create.

To complete the experience requires that it take place in a context. If the experience takes place in the normal context of feeding egos or seeking pleasure it will be an empty and meaningless moment, full of sentiment or fantasy, but offering no real intimacy or enduring satisfaction.

By contrast, when the experience takes place in a context of innocent consciousness and caring, then both people are aware of their own hunger, the hunger of the other person, and the pure joy of providing for each other a richly personal and ultimately satisfying intimate experience.

Consciousness and caring are also protective in that no one ever needs to feel afraid to show that he/she is internally hungry. Too often, in normal relationships between lovers, or between parents and children, people are humiliated or even exploited for allowing their internal hungers to show—like their innocent desire for personal conversation and conscious touch.

Is it becoming apparent that mastering *personal conversation* and *conscious touch* is critical to *building bonded relationships*? In the next chapter, we complete the requirements for building emotional bonds by defining everyone's internal need to *share reality, purposes, and quintessential moments.*

Sharing Reality, Purposes, & Quintessential Moments

The key element to creating intimacy in any relationship is becoming competent to share, and *sharing reality* is the most crucial experience in forming an emotional bond. By contrast, *arguing* about reality is the most common method for creating distance between couples, parents and children, and friends. The reason people often get mired in needless arguments is they define reality in terms of ideas, beliefs, and feelings, rather than by observing everyday facts.

If people define reality by observing facts, they can acknowledge and understand each other's perspectives. Everyone has a mental and emotional need to share reality, but to feed this need people must define reality based on *observations,* **not** *judgments, beliefs, or feelings.*

One of the many reasons that my parents and I never shared a single intimate moment in over fifty years of knowing each other was the fact that we could not share reality. A striking example occurred in my thirties, when my mother made a comment about my teen-age years. The *fact* was that in high school, I was always in honors classes, never earned a grade below a B, participated in two sports (cross country and wrestling), had two jobs, paid for everything except basic room and board, did all the outside chores for the house, patio, and garage, and never got into any teen-age trouble.

In commenting about me as a teenager, my mother said, "*We always wanted to approve of you—you just never did anything we could approve of!*" When she made this observation, I already had a rule for responding to criticism*, never explain*, but I had not yet mastered exploring those criticisms to discover their sources in beliefs and feelings.

Instead, I froze for a moment, paralyzed by disbelief. Thinking about it later, I could see that part of my mother's statement came from her lack of self-worth, which made her too fragile to accept a shred of responsibility, for anything, ever. In addition, she *believed* that I did not respect or appreciate her contribution to my life, and her *feelings* were hurt that I never asked for any material thing after the age of 13.

Of course, the demands of her insecure ego, as well as her beliefs and feelings were all unconscious, so she could not acknowledge or discuss any issue with the purpose of wanting to understand. Instead, from her perspective no one else had a perspective, so it never crossed her mind that anything beyond her beliefs and feelings even existed.

Internal Development

The principle of life here is that without internal development people cannot see reality accurately, and as a result, cannot consciously share experience or acknowledge someone else's perspective. Many skills are required for people to create intimacy, and the lack of internal skill is at the root of all dissatisfaction in intimate relationships—mates, parents and children, and friends.

To discover the role of sharing reality in your life, observe how you relate to your mate, children and friends, and discover to what degree you have the skill to both acknowledge and understand the experiences and perspective of each person. Also, note how much you rely on *observation* to define your *picture of reality*, and to what degree you rely on *judgments, beliefs, and feelings.* Next, bring to mind old conflicts and note how often you and the other person created competing pictures of reality that were responsible for the disagreement.

For contrast, observe moments of intimacy, warmth, and connection, and see how often a *shared reality* was at least partly responsible. Sharing judgments, beliefs, or feelings may create temporary *feelings* of intimacy, but sow the seeds for future disillusion and conflict because judgments eventually diverge, and when that happens, it creates a gulf we cannot bridge.

Conversely, if our observations diverge, but we share a *purpose of wanting to understand*, we can still build a bridge to each other. We build this bridge with the competence to understand our own and the other person's perspective.

Another reality people more often *argue* about than *share* is *responsibility.* With normal training, everyone believes that if he experiences mental and emotional pain then someone else—a mate, child, or friend—is responsible. The reason for the pain may be anything—time together, attention, money, sex, chores, child-care or child rearing. What is virtually the same in every normal conflict is disagreement on the *reality* of *what happened*, who is *responsible,* or both.

The most effective and permanent fix for these arguments is for each person to take complete responsibility for all his own pain. This includes giving up all *rights to fairness*! The combination of taking responsibility for every pain, and never expecting life or relationships to be fair, creates expectations that are congruent with the facts of reality. Once two people are conscious, competent, and perfectly responsible, they are internally prepared to grow, give, and share.

If my mother had wanted to see reality accurately, we could have acknowledged the facts, identified both her and my responses, and come to understand each other's experiences and perspective. Instead, it was impossible to share or discuss anything when she assumed that I was responsible for pains she could not define. To varying degrees, most people with normal training develop a *vested interest* in twisting reality to justify their distorted feelings and beliefs.

Becoming competent to see and share reality is not a small task. In fact, it is a huge task. This is why you must consciously master the developmental task of learning how to *think for understanding*. Here, you learn to *concentrate on one issue at a time, make observations, ask questions, define words, see details, identify similarities and differences, describe content, and understand process.* Each mental tool is necessary to make your mind a *functional working consciousness,* rather than the normal barely functioning *unconscious reaction machine.*

Once you have mastered thinking for understanding, then you are prepared to develop self-worth and feed internal needs. It is imperative that you master these developmental tasks so you learn how to take internal responsibility, and over time, become competent to grow, give, and share with another person.

One reason people experience difficulty in building bonded relationships is that no one receives the specific internal training necessary to become a conscious, caring, and competent human being. Without mastering exploring for understanding and feeding internal needs, we have no more chance to build a bonded relationship than we do to create an individual life that is fulfilled and meaningful.

Conscious Purposes

After learning how to share reality, the next task is to define *conscious purposes.* Normally, we fail to consciously define our life's purposes. Instead, we complain about what we do **not** want, rather than clearly define what we ***do*** want. As a result, we often meander through life reacting to daily events without direction or purpose. Supported only by an evaluative attitude, we may be unhappy with the status quo, but still fail to define a *conscious purpose.* We only know that somehow, someone, or perhaps just life has failed to provide the fulfillment that we expected.

Everyone needs to replace *unconscious reactions* with well defined *conscious purposes.* The most critical is to acquire a whole-hearted commitment to master every *responsibility*—for ourselves alone, and in relationships with other people. This requires we master thinking for understanding and feeding internal needs. Without internal development, we bring a child's perspective to adult relationships. Eventually, our *responsibilities exceed our competence.* One result is that enduring intimacy and genuine fulfillment are forever beyond our developmental capacity.

Adult bonded relationships require both *equality* and *reciprocity*. Consequently, in all romantic relationships it is important that people share a *conscious purpose* to fulfill their internal potentials and build internal happiness. One life-affirming consequence is that a conscious couple purposefully learns how to feed their minds truth and senses beauty. In sharing truth and beauty, each moment becomes a *primal experience.*

As we have seen, *primal* means not only do our minds, emotions, and senses *work*, but they work in *harmony* with each other. Sharing primal experience means that you and your mate experience life intensely, in part, by innocently receiving and honestly responding to every moment.

Quintessential Moments

When primal experience becomes an everyday habit, couples are prepared to add a *conscious purpose* to share *quintessential moments* to their list of priorities. In normal life, quintessential moments are largely accidental. Sharing a sunset, sex, buying a new car or house, or being present at a birth or death can feel like a quintessential moment, and may be. The problem is that with normal training, we fail to distinguish between *unconsciously reacting* to stimulation or pleasure, and *purposefully creating and consciously responding* to real love, timeless truth, and innocent beauty.

It is not helpful to evaluate or judge each other's experiences to determine whether they qualify as *quintessential.* Instead, simply master the internal needs and potentials, as well as thinking for understanding and building emotional bonds, and you will experience for yourself precisely what defines a quintessential moment.

As you can see, building bonded relationships requires that we integrate the complex developmental skills and awareness presented here in this book, and in my other book, **Expressing Love—Pursuing Truth—Experiencing Beauty:** *Timeless Steps to the Ultimate Satisfaction—A Meaningful Life.* Together these two books provide the information every person needs to create the ultimate satisfaction—a meaningful life.

If you would like to learn more about the **Center for Mental & Emotional Development** (CMED), and the ongoing training program for becoming loving & wise so you can build internal happiness, please visit my web site:

www.paulhatherley.com